Art Mandala Coloring Book

Copyright: Published in the United States by Lora Frierson
Published January 2017
ISBN-13: 978-1542520225
ISBN-10: 1542520223

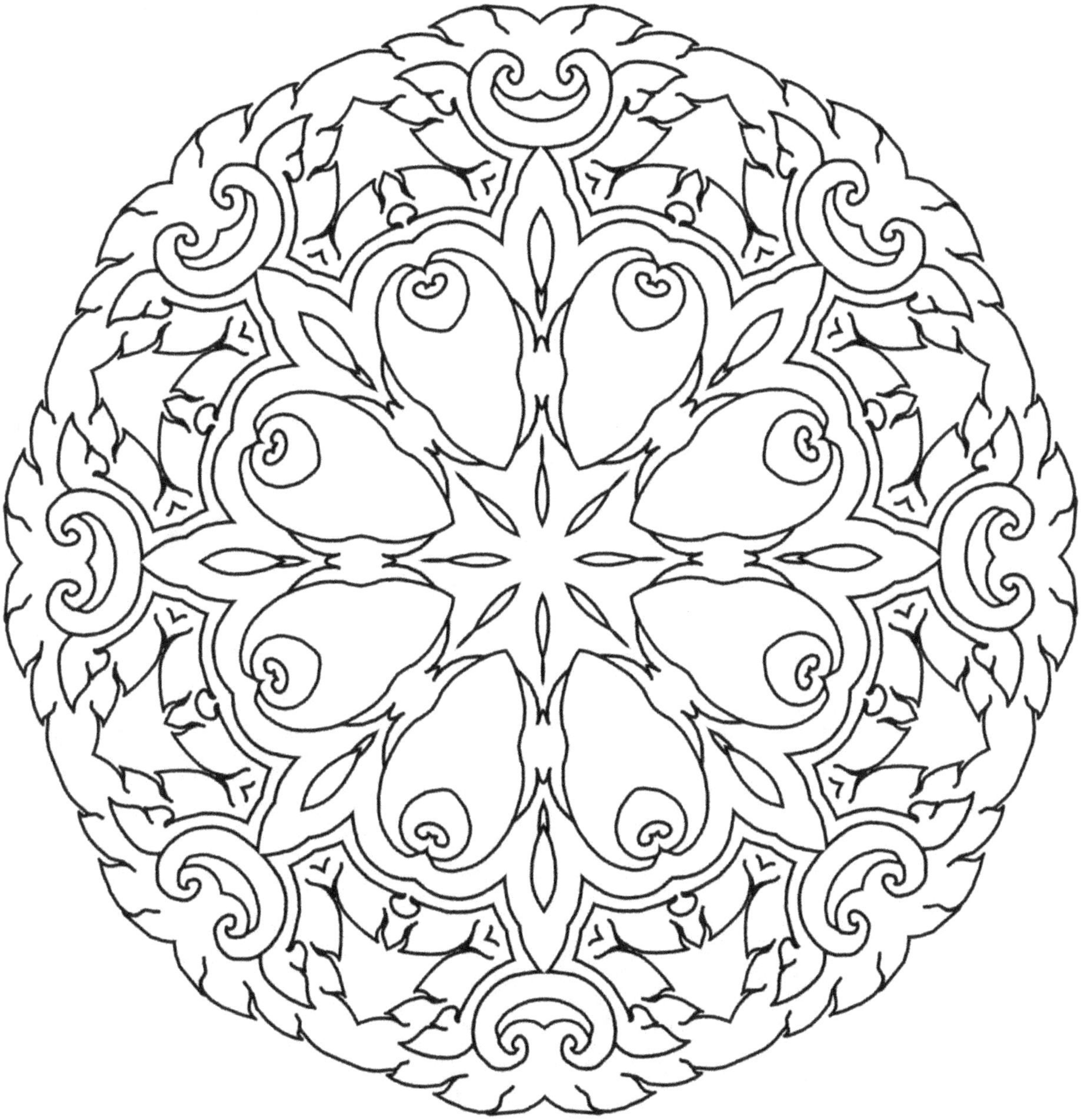

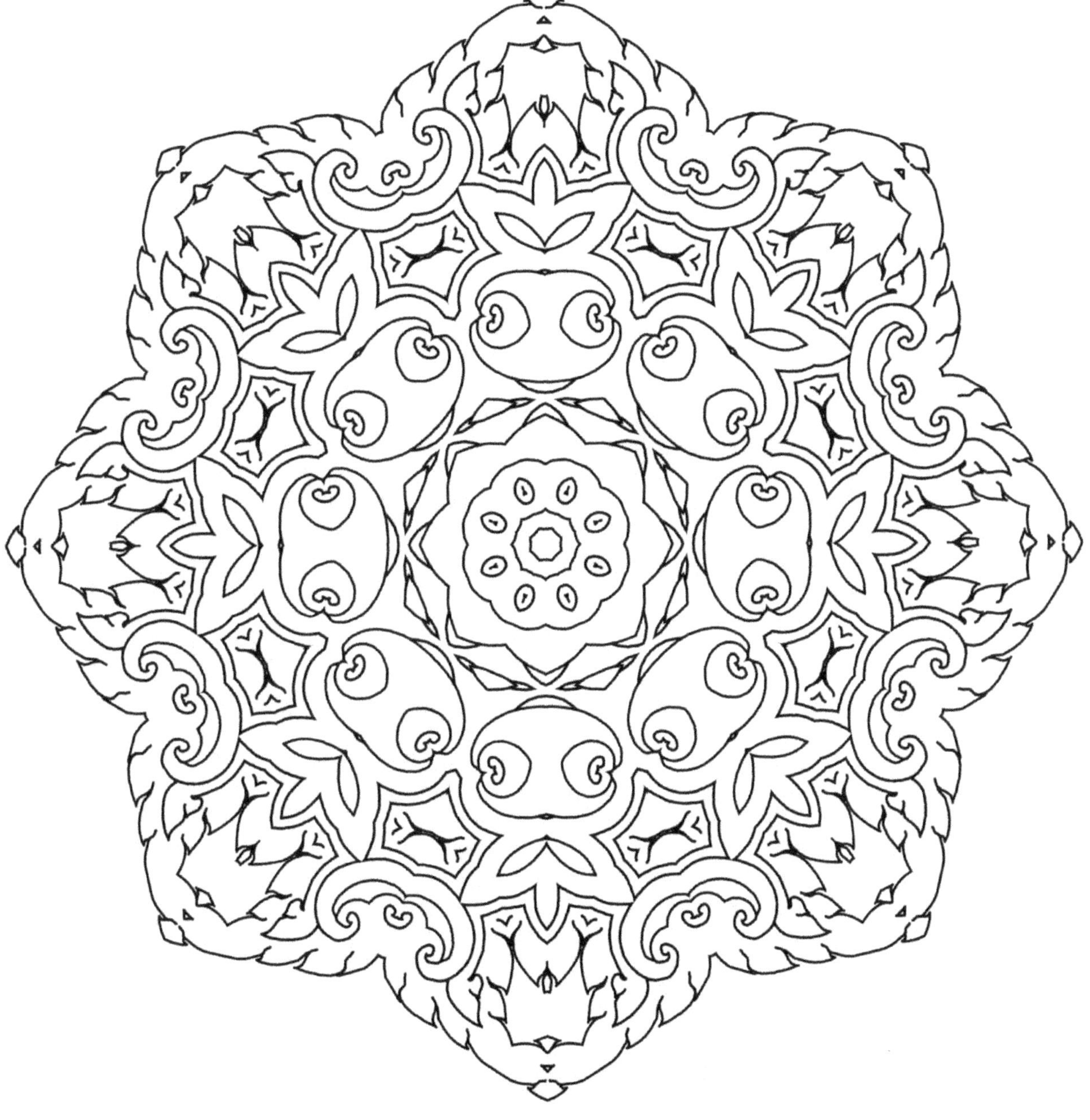

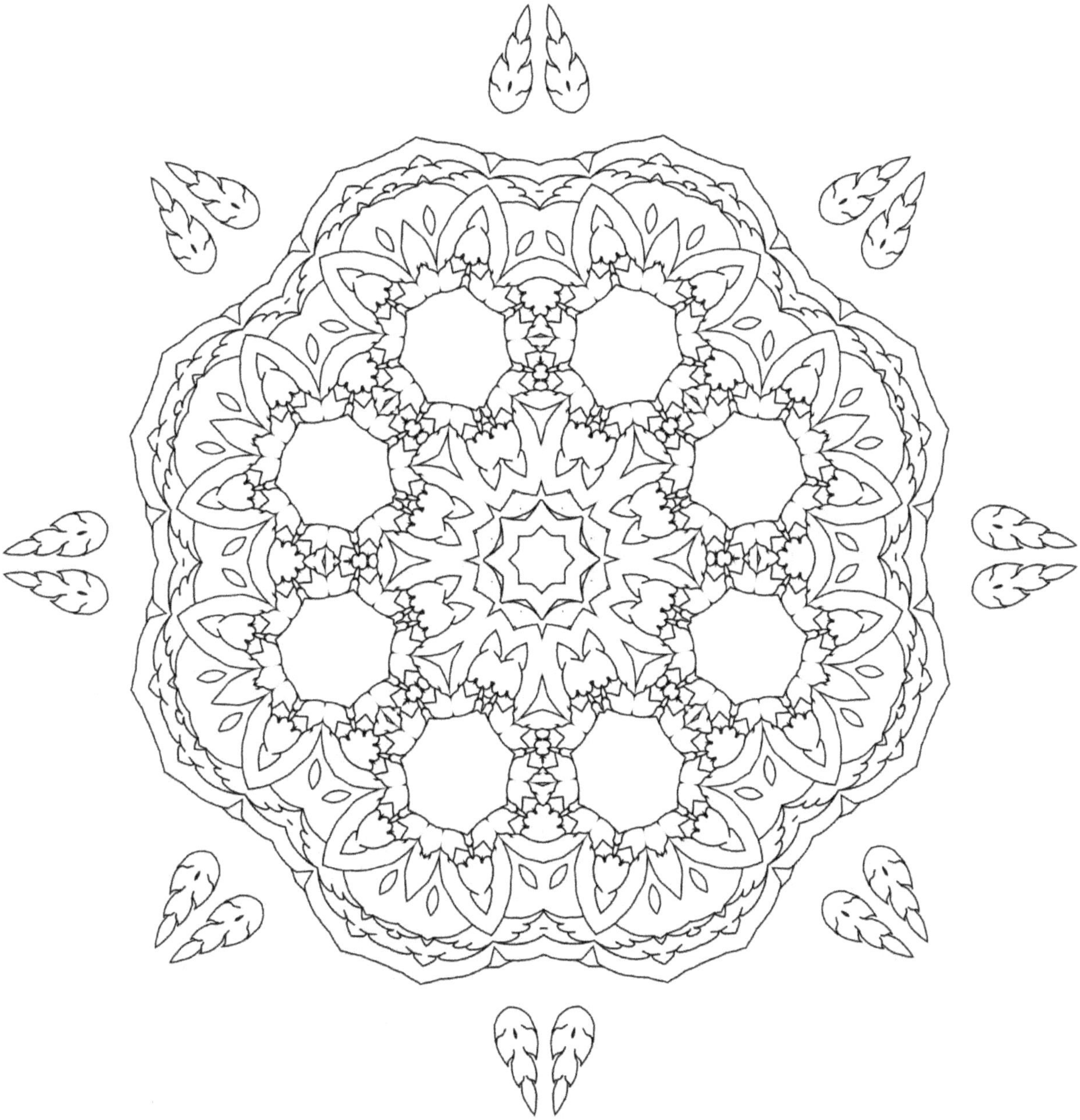

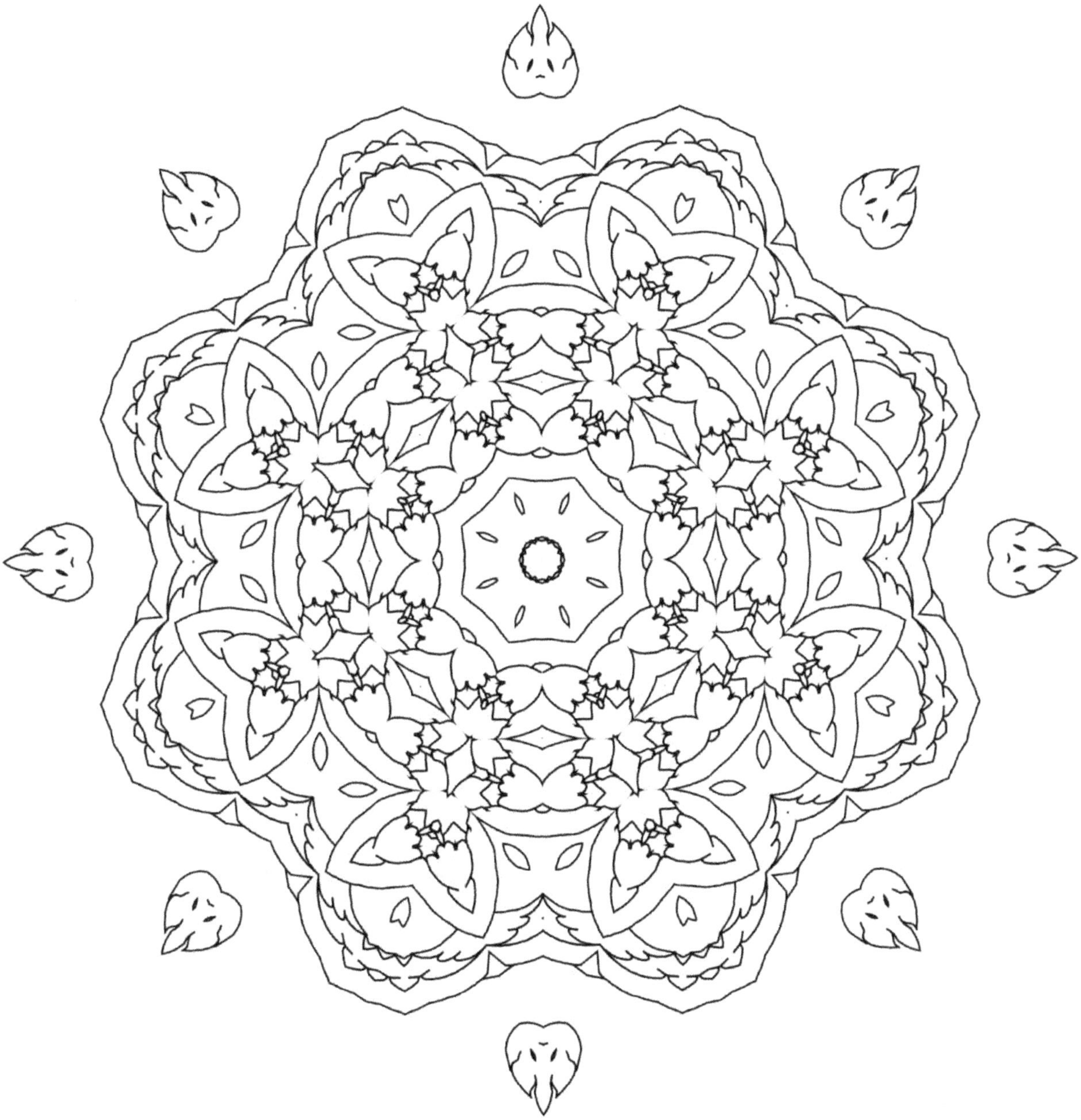

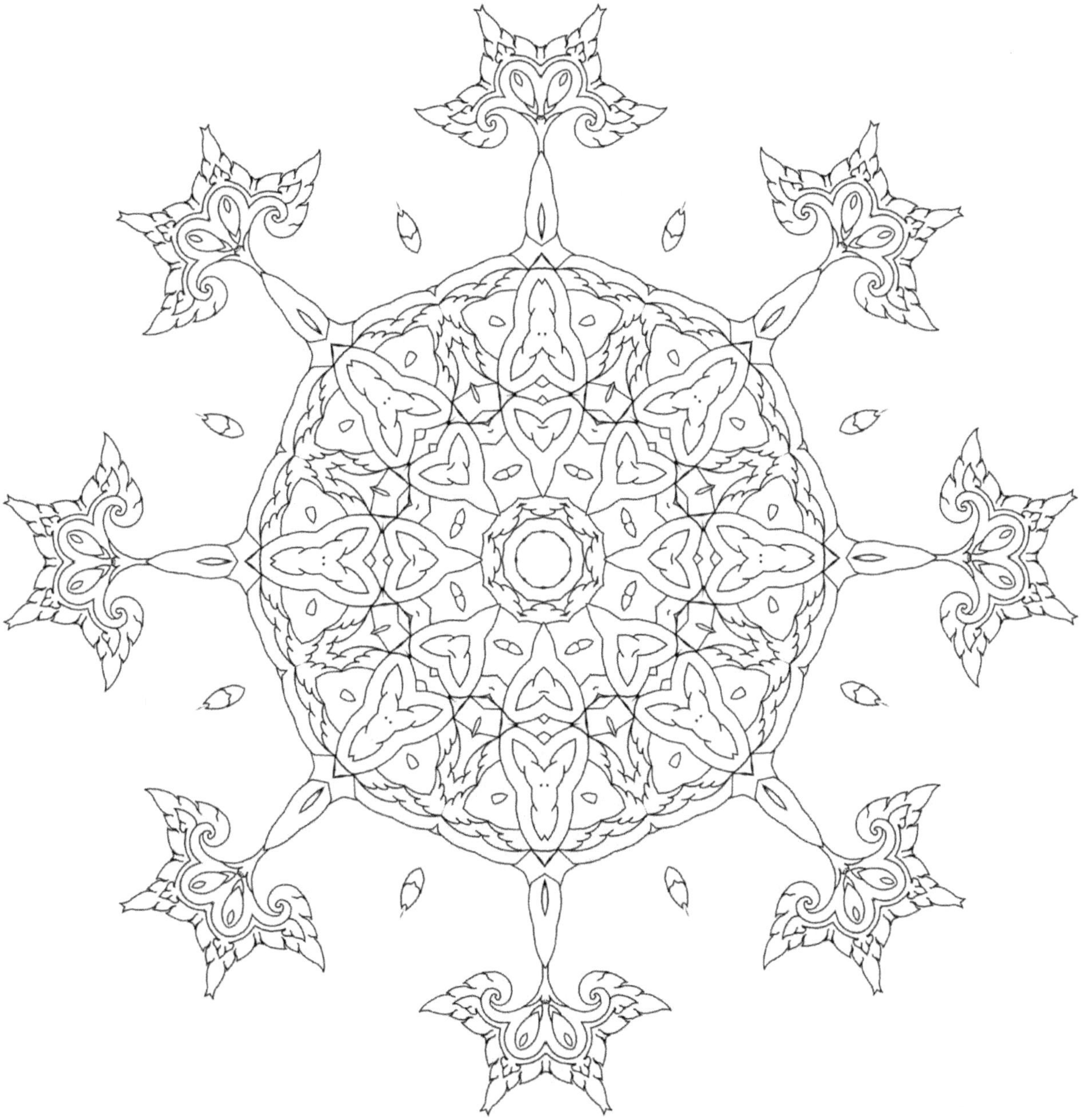

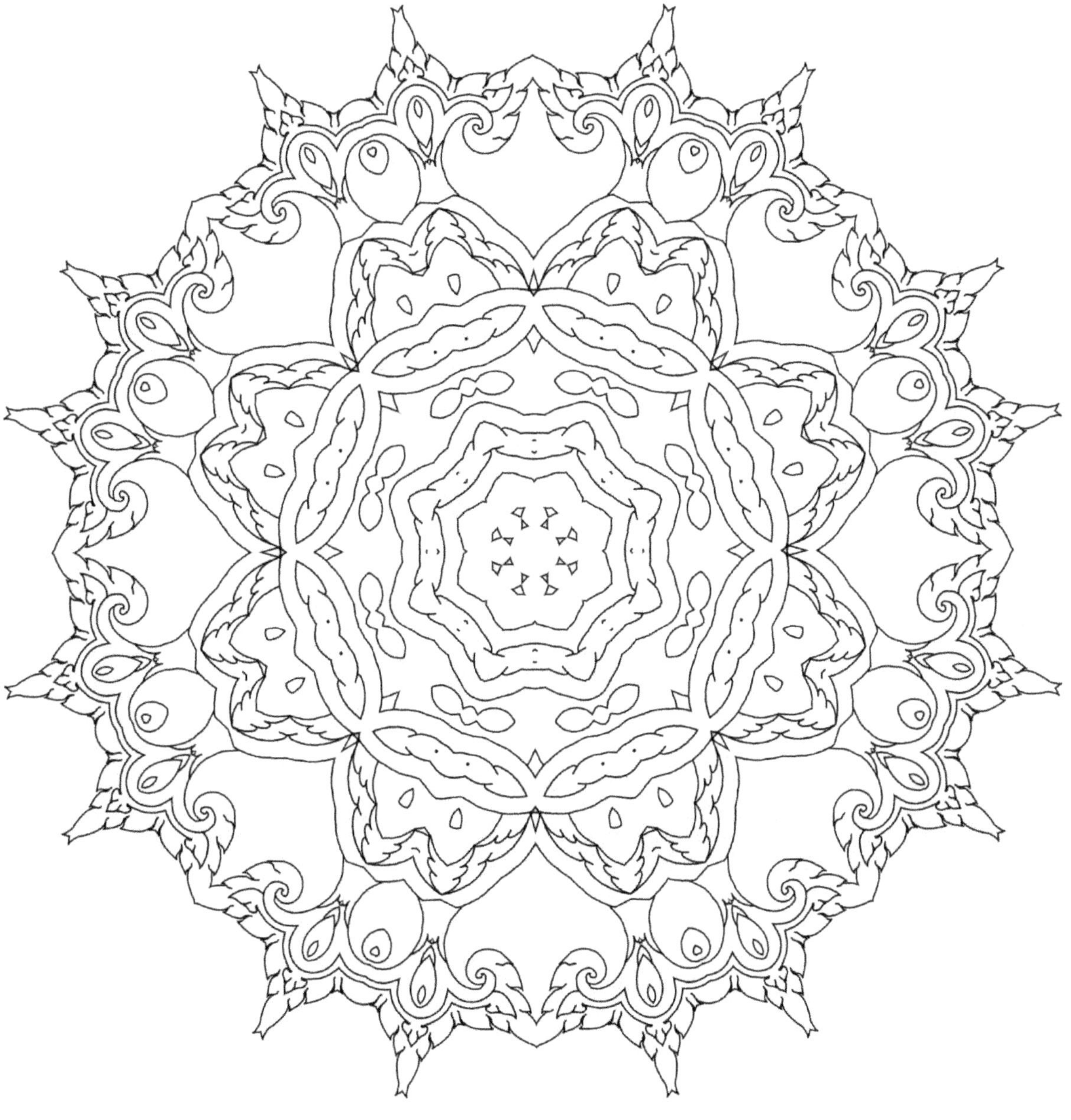

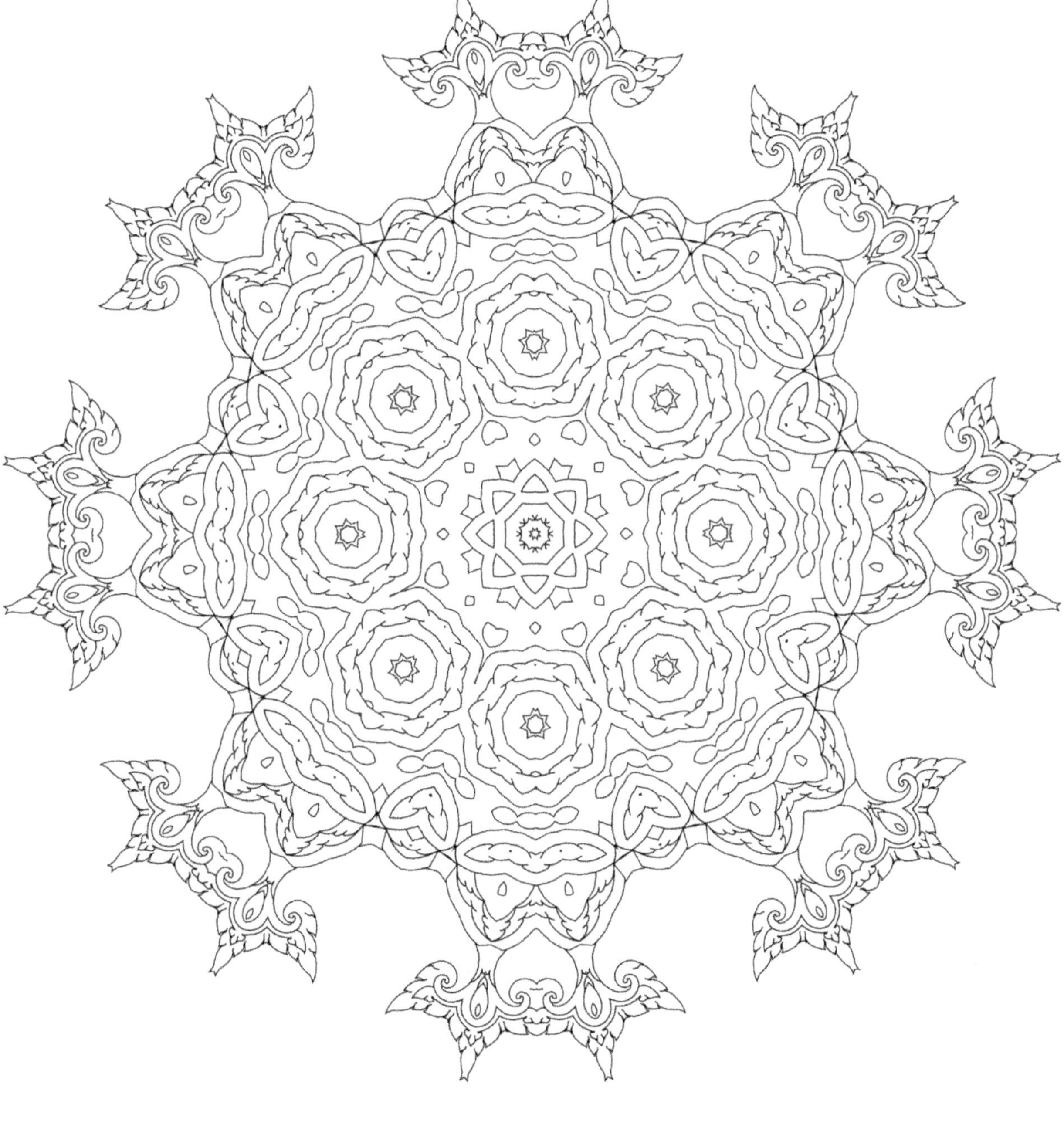

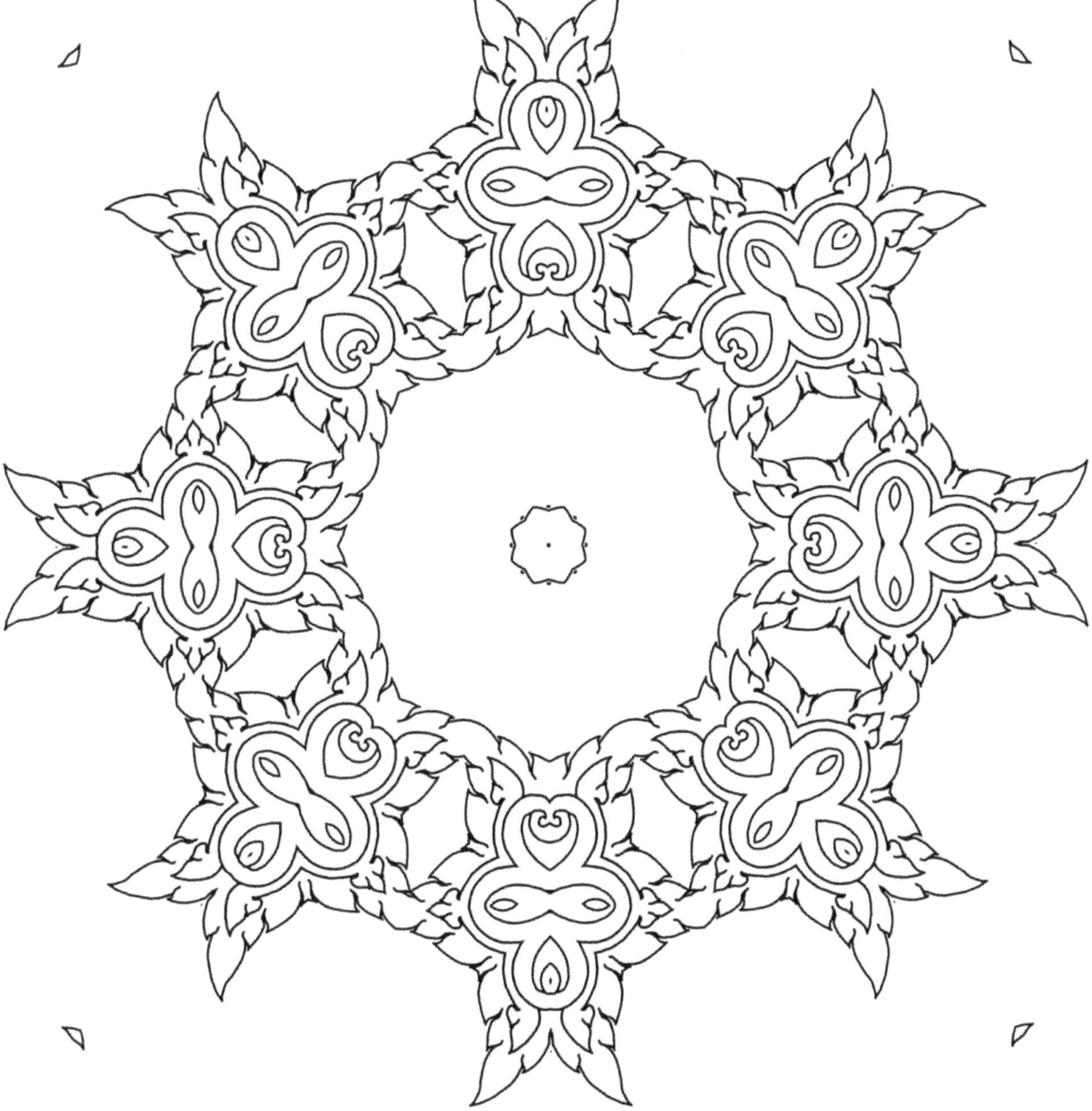

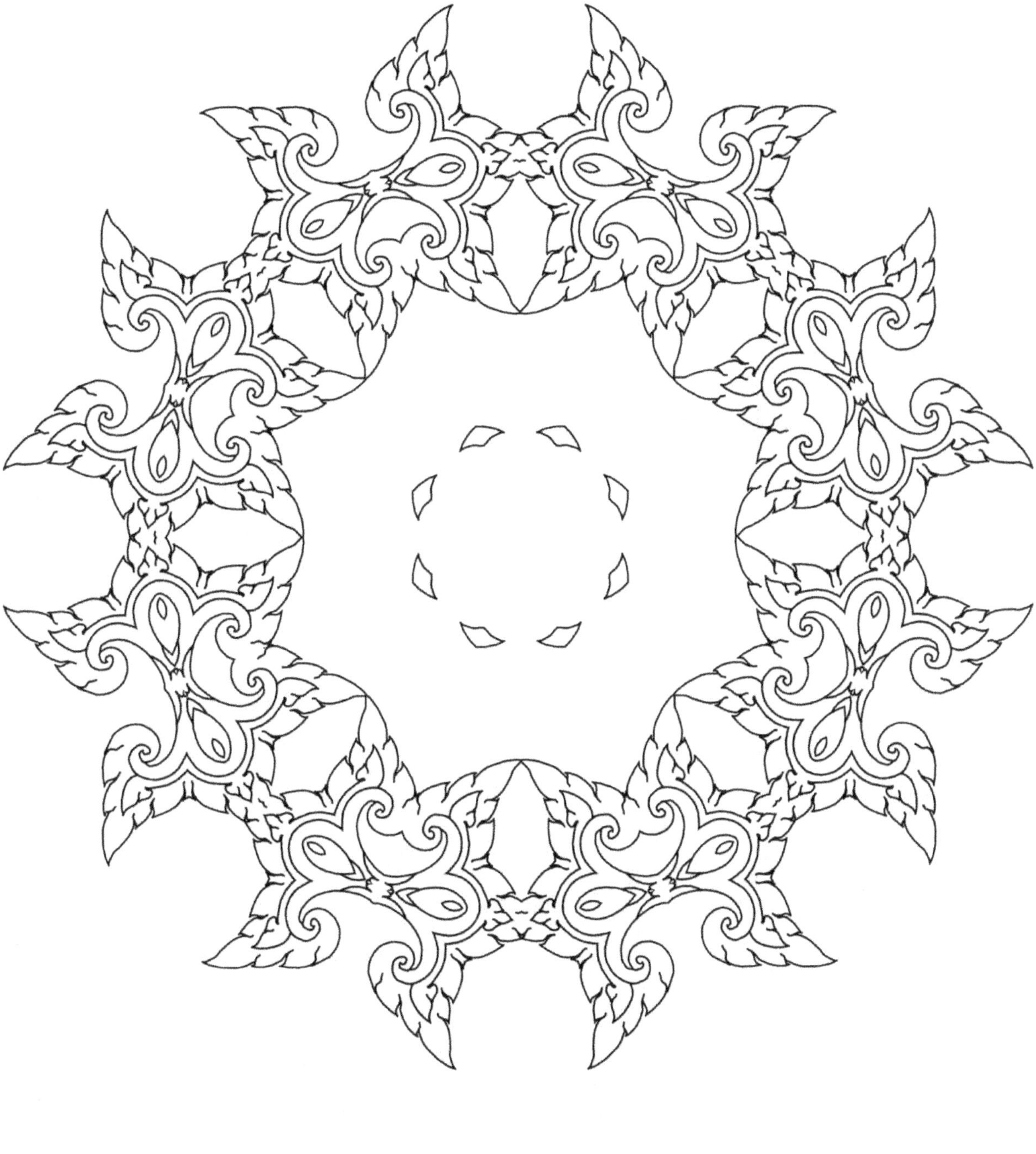

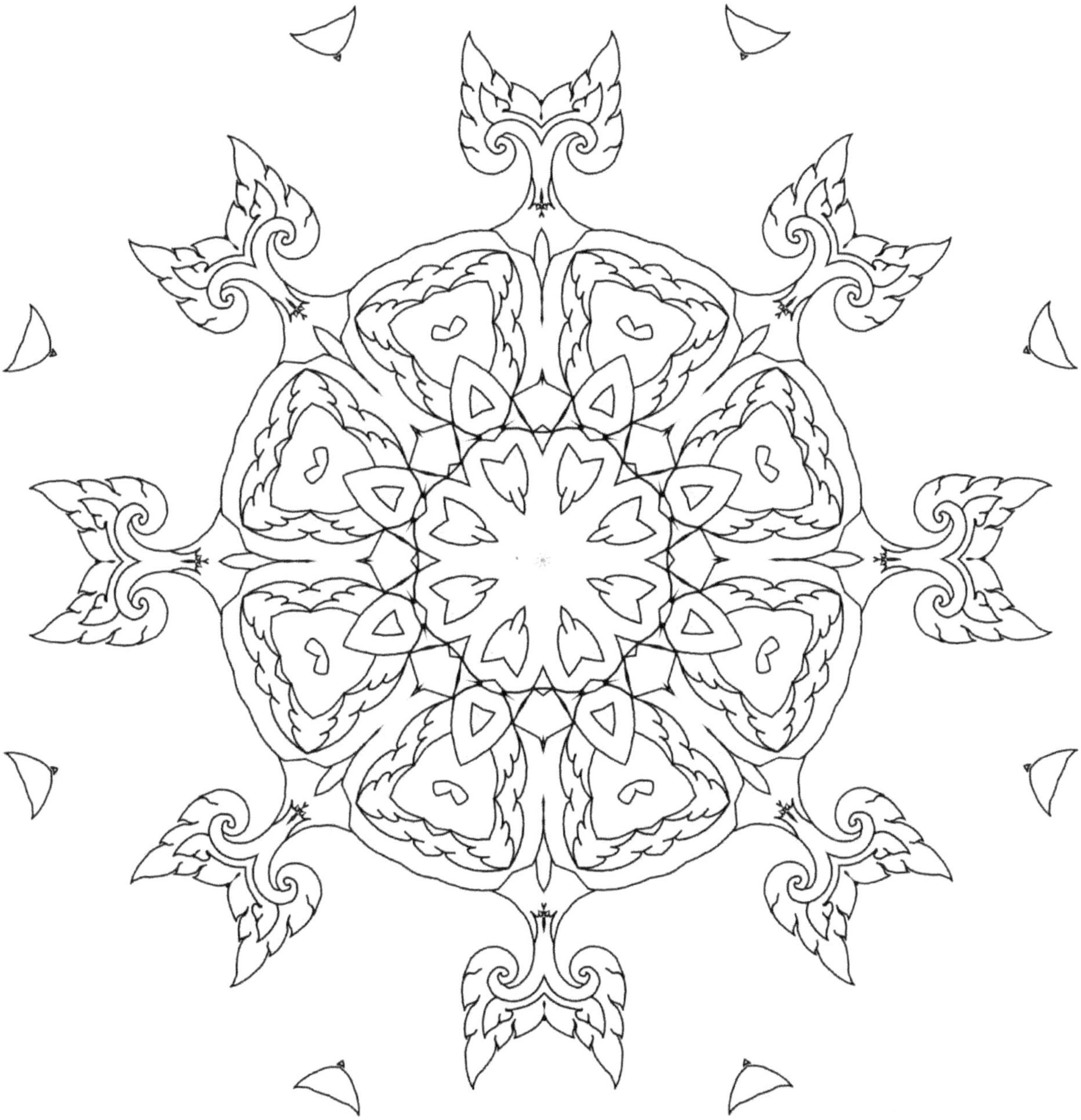

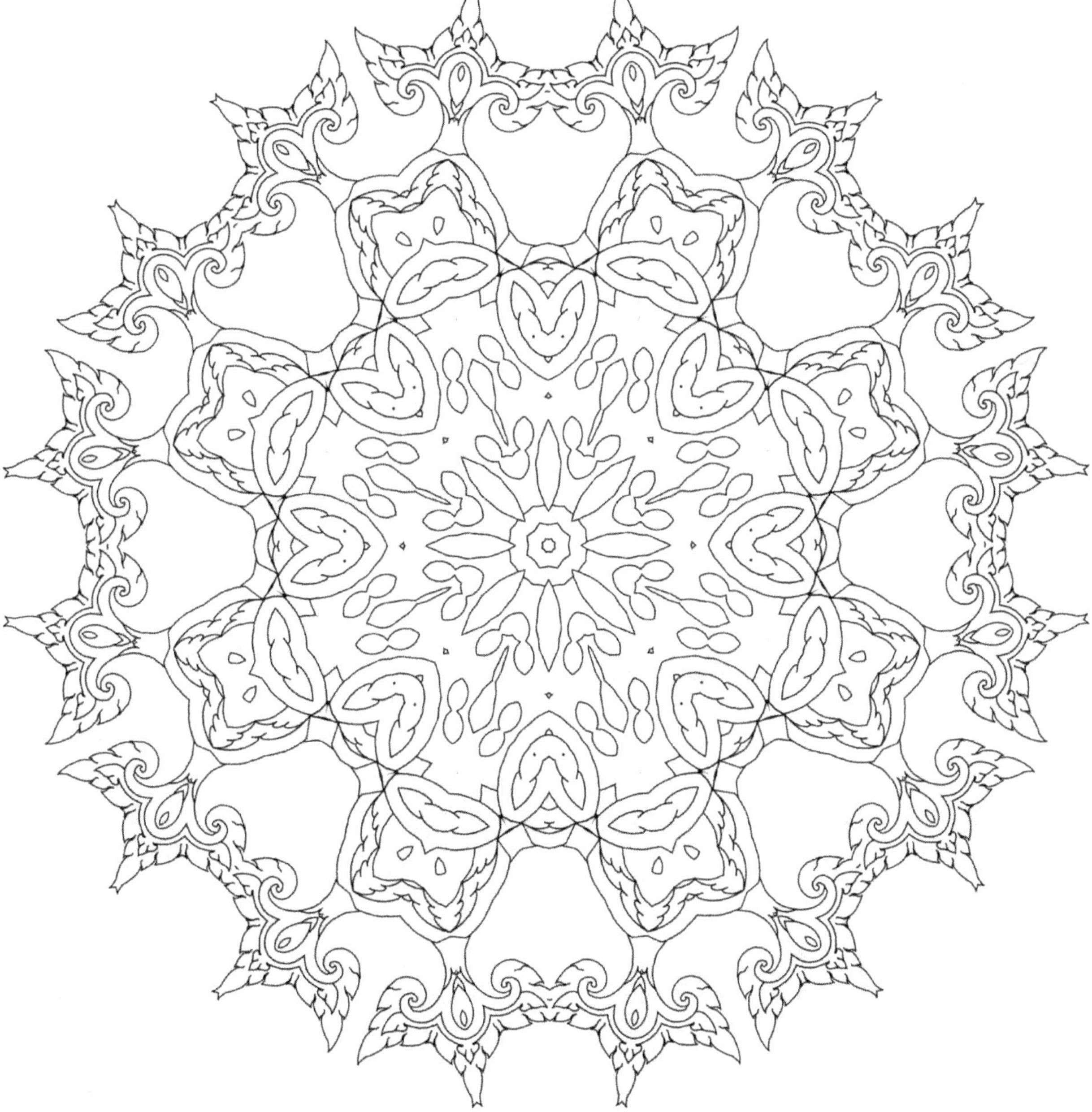

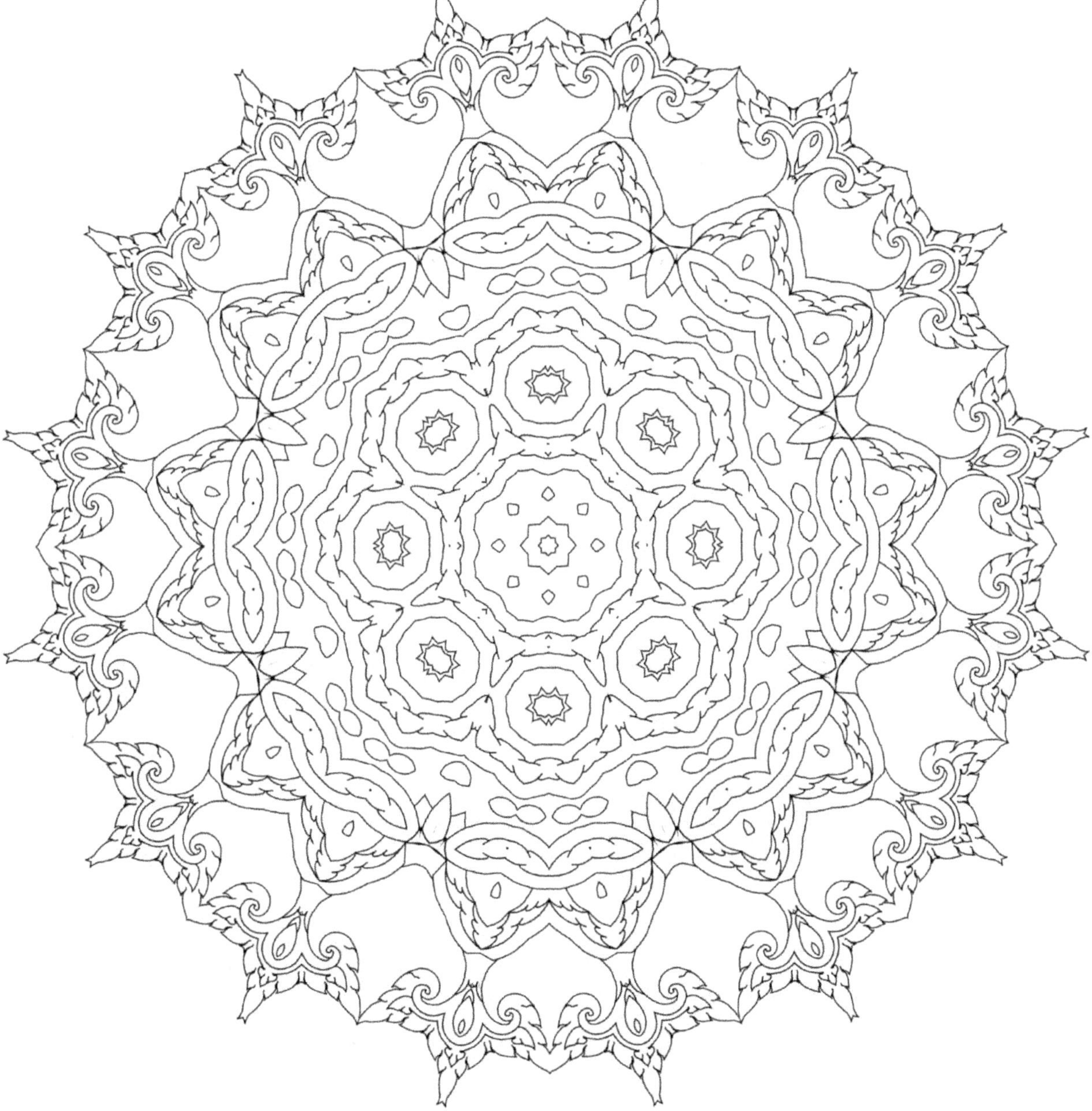

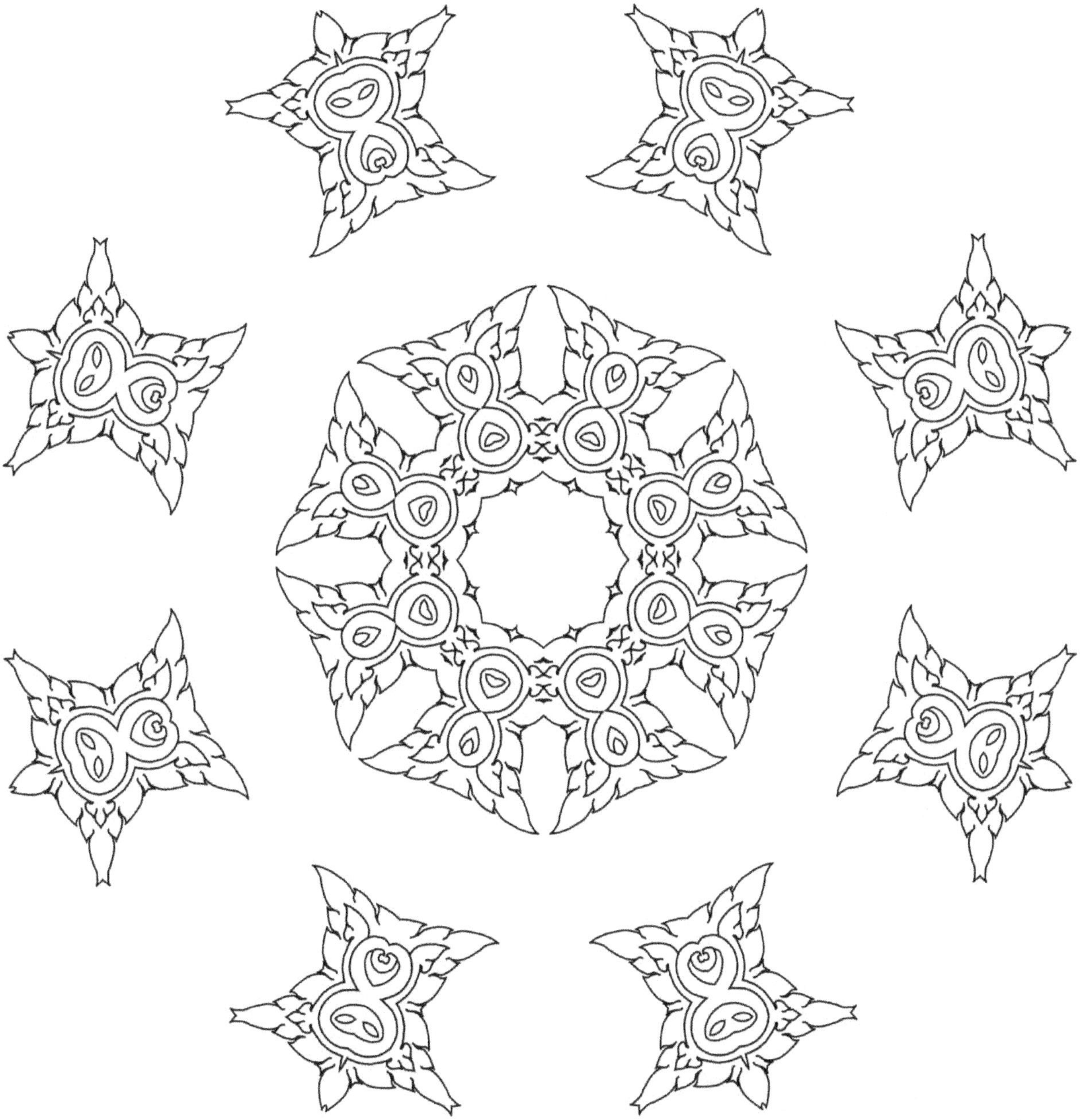

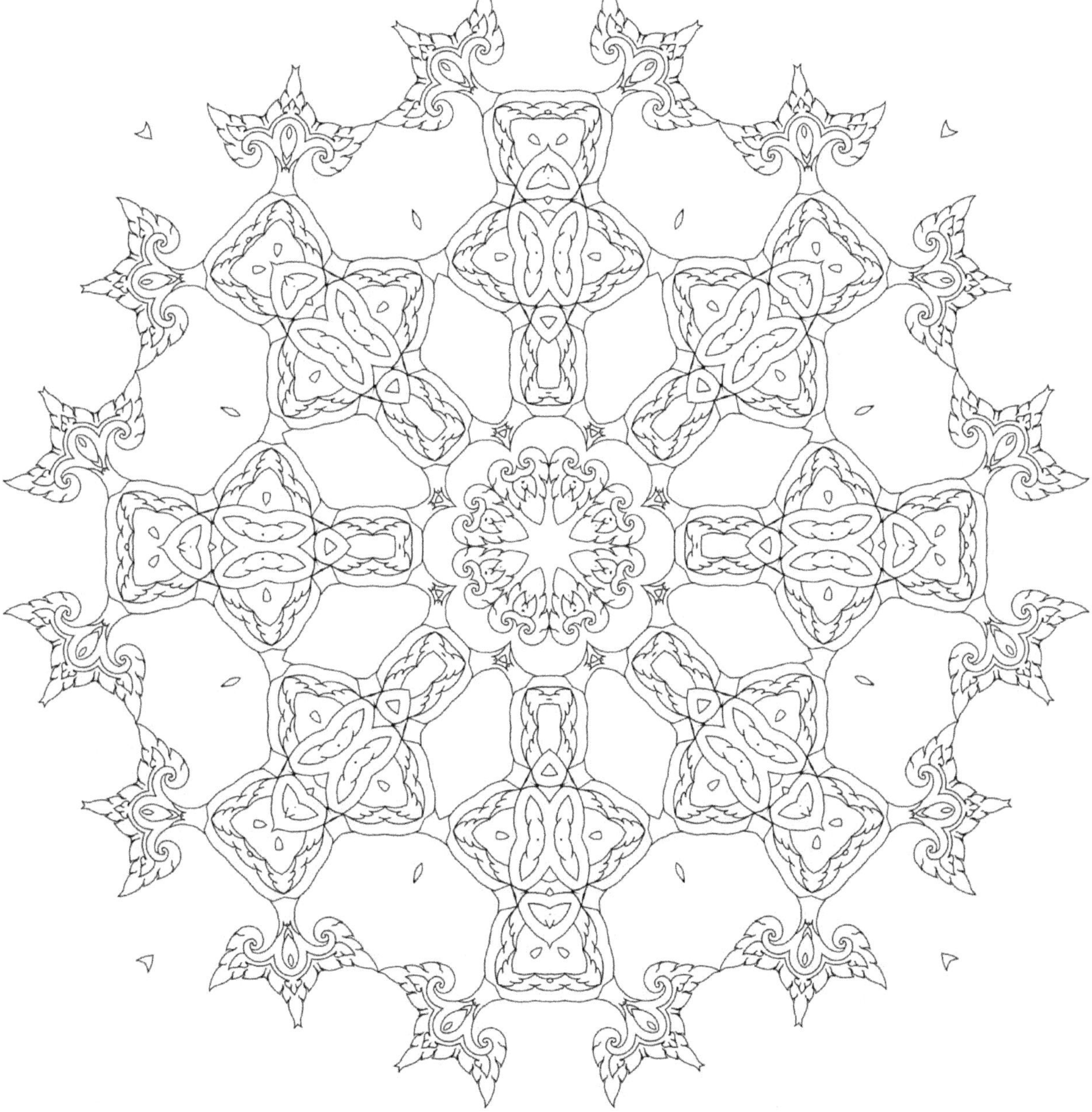

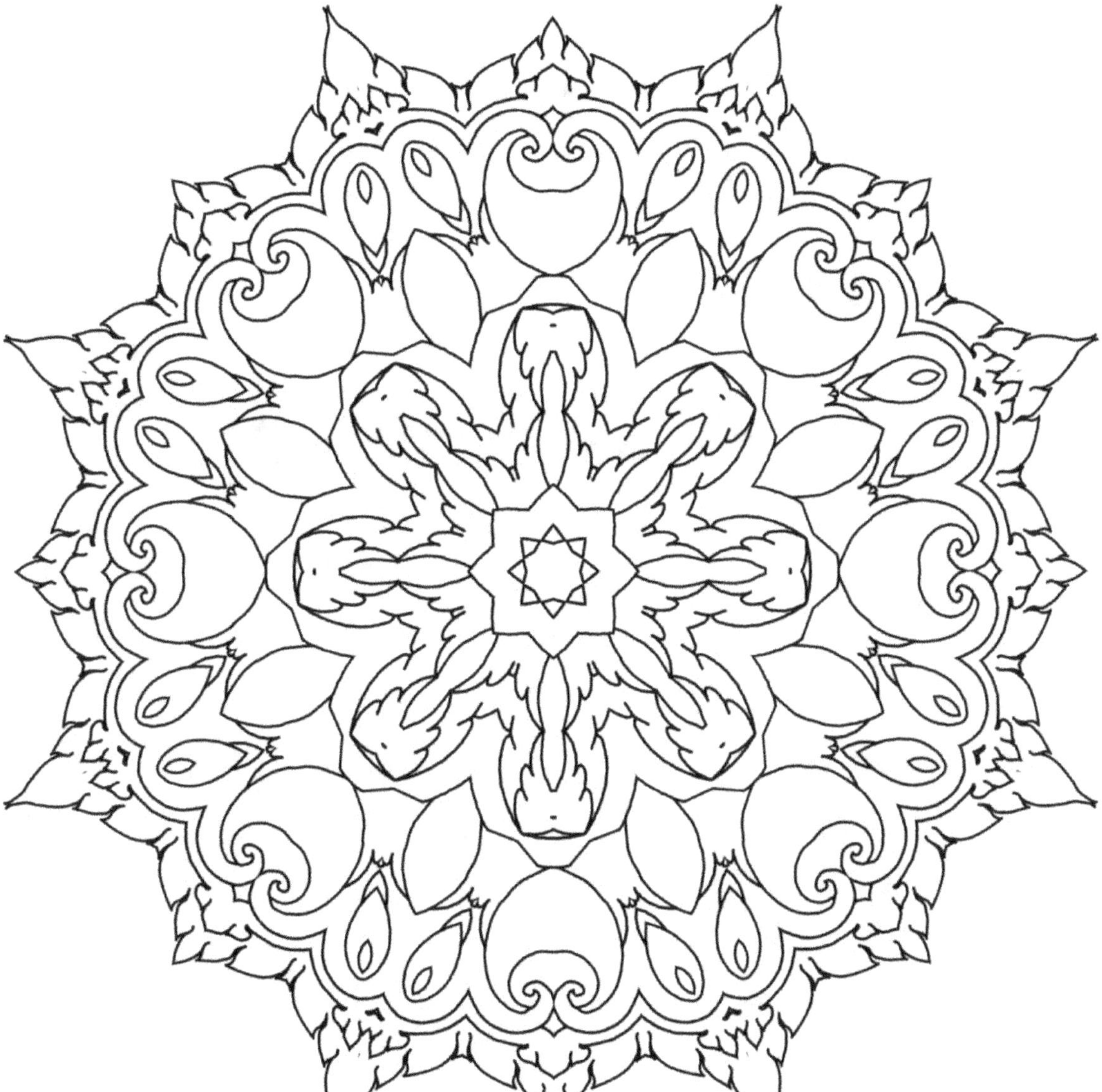

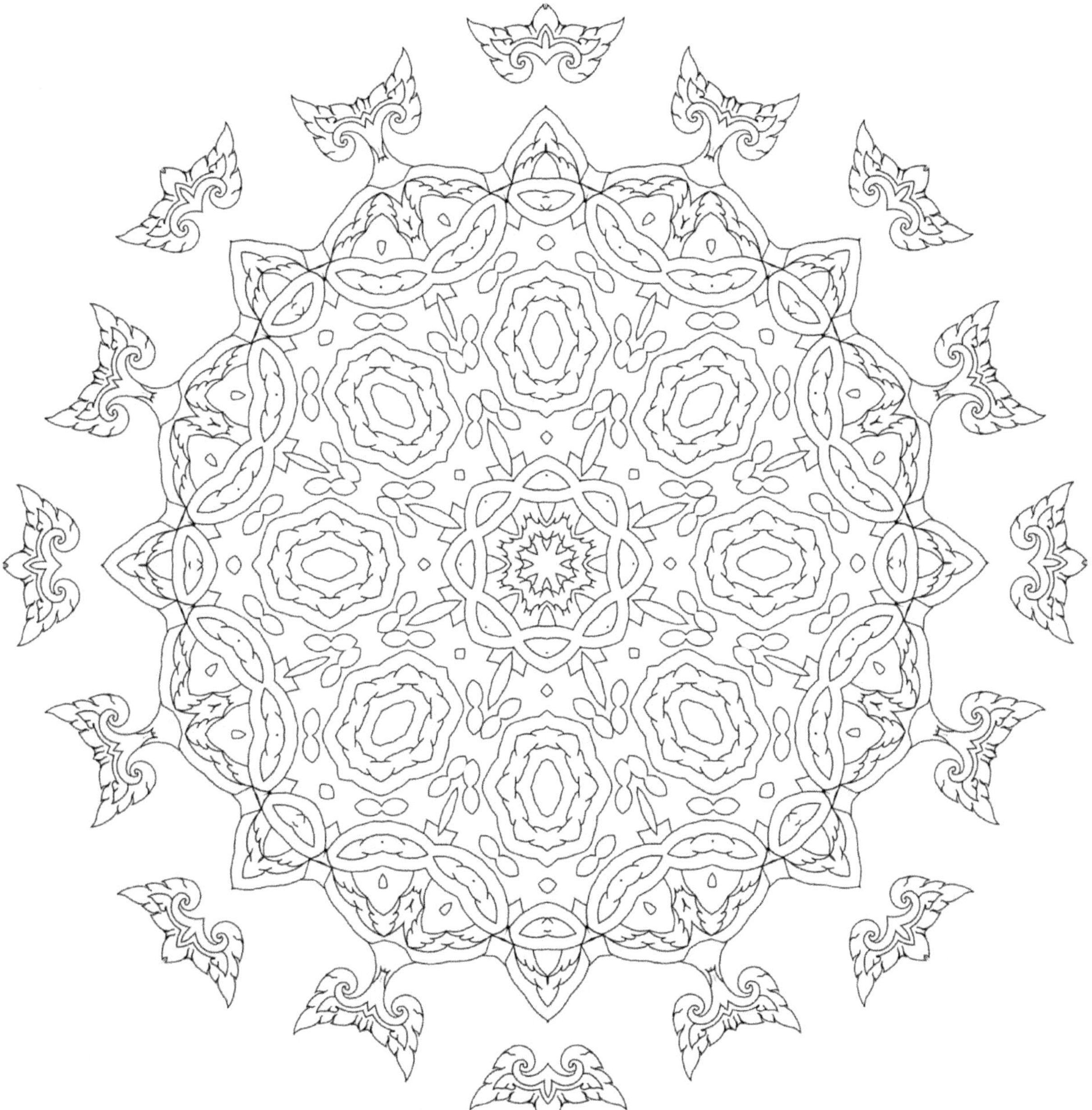

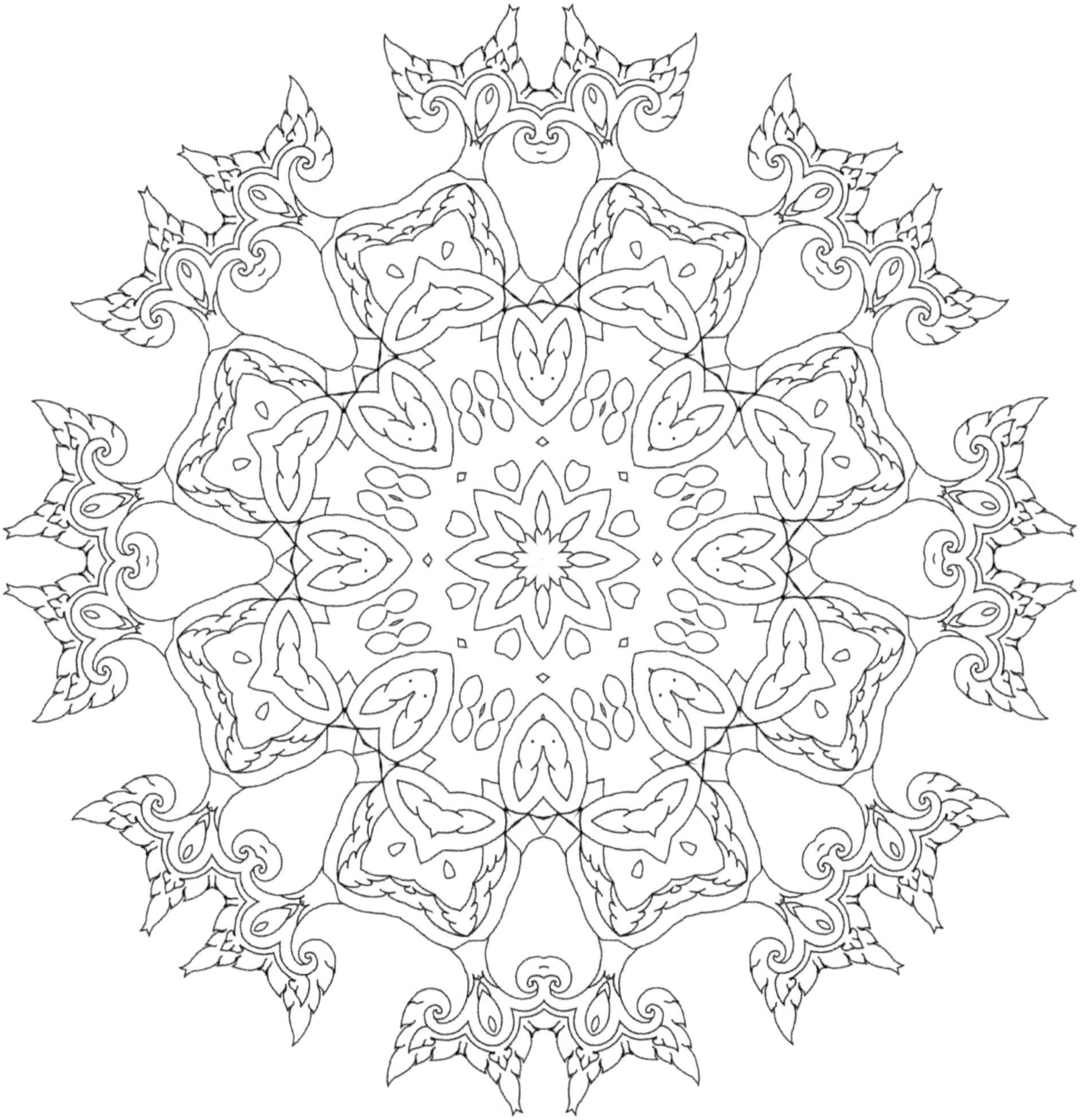

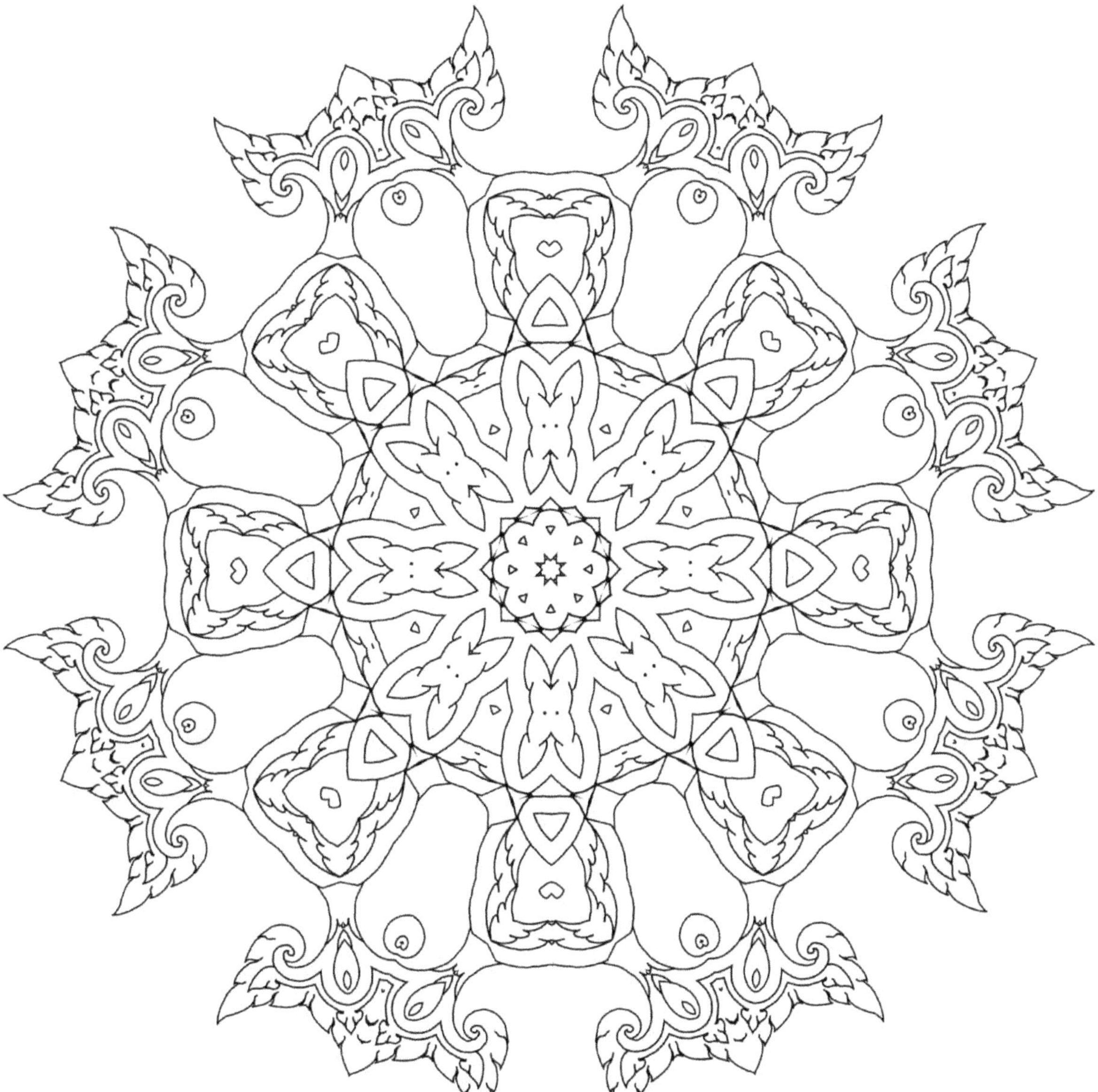

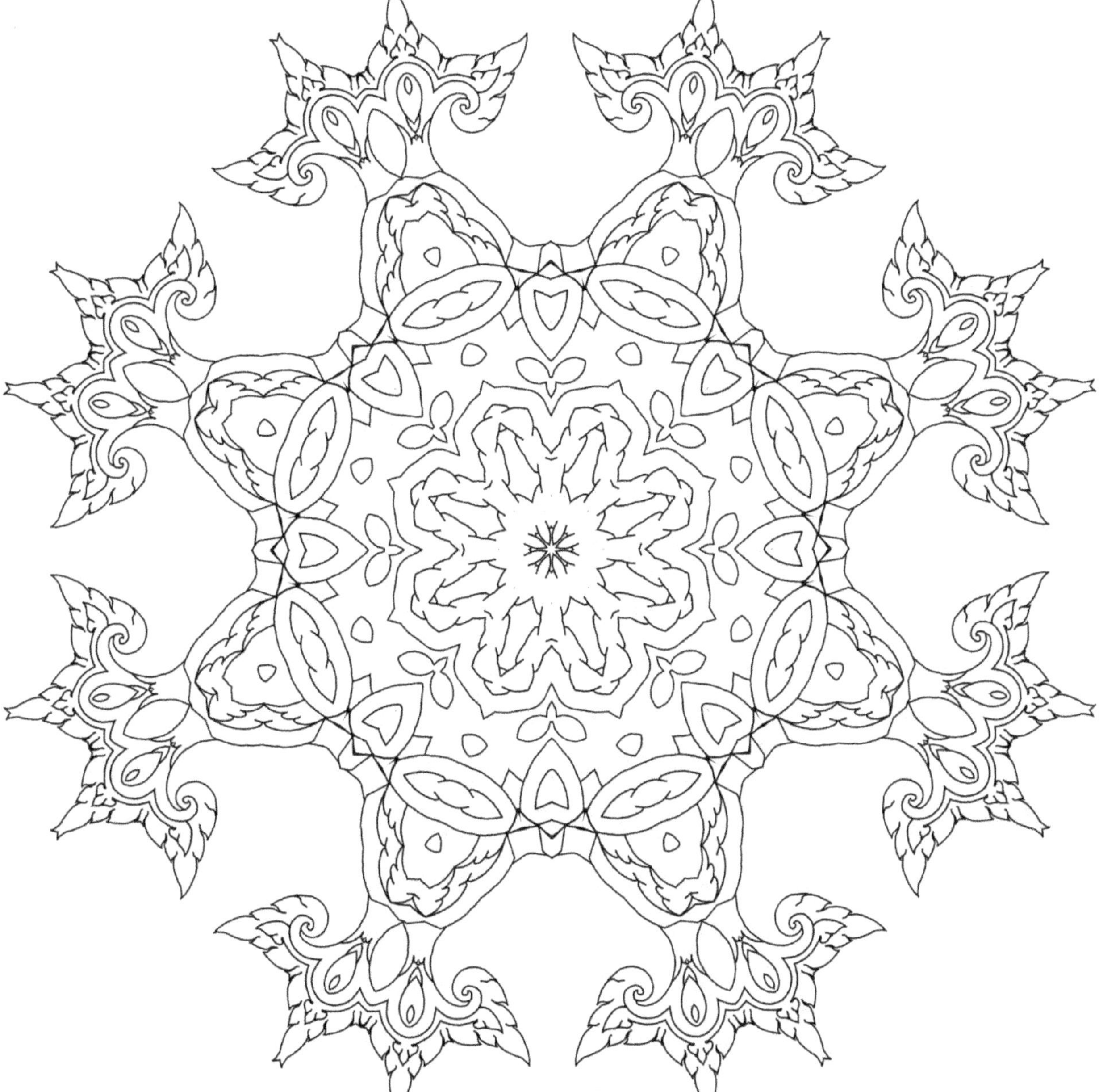

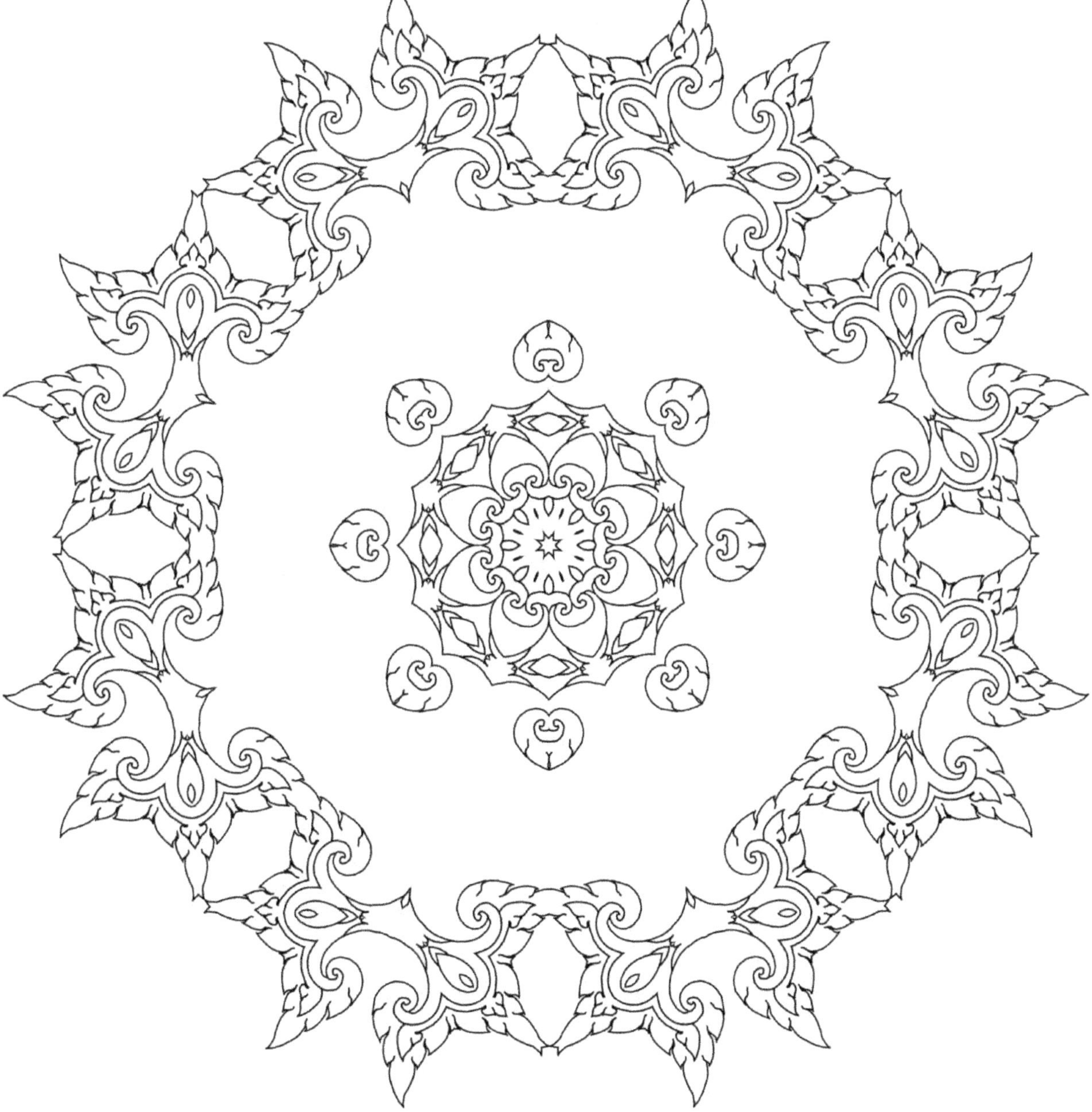

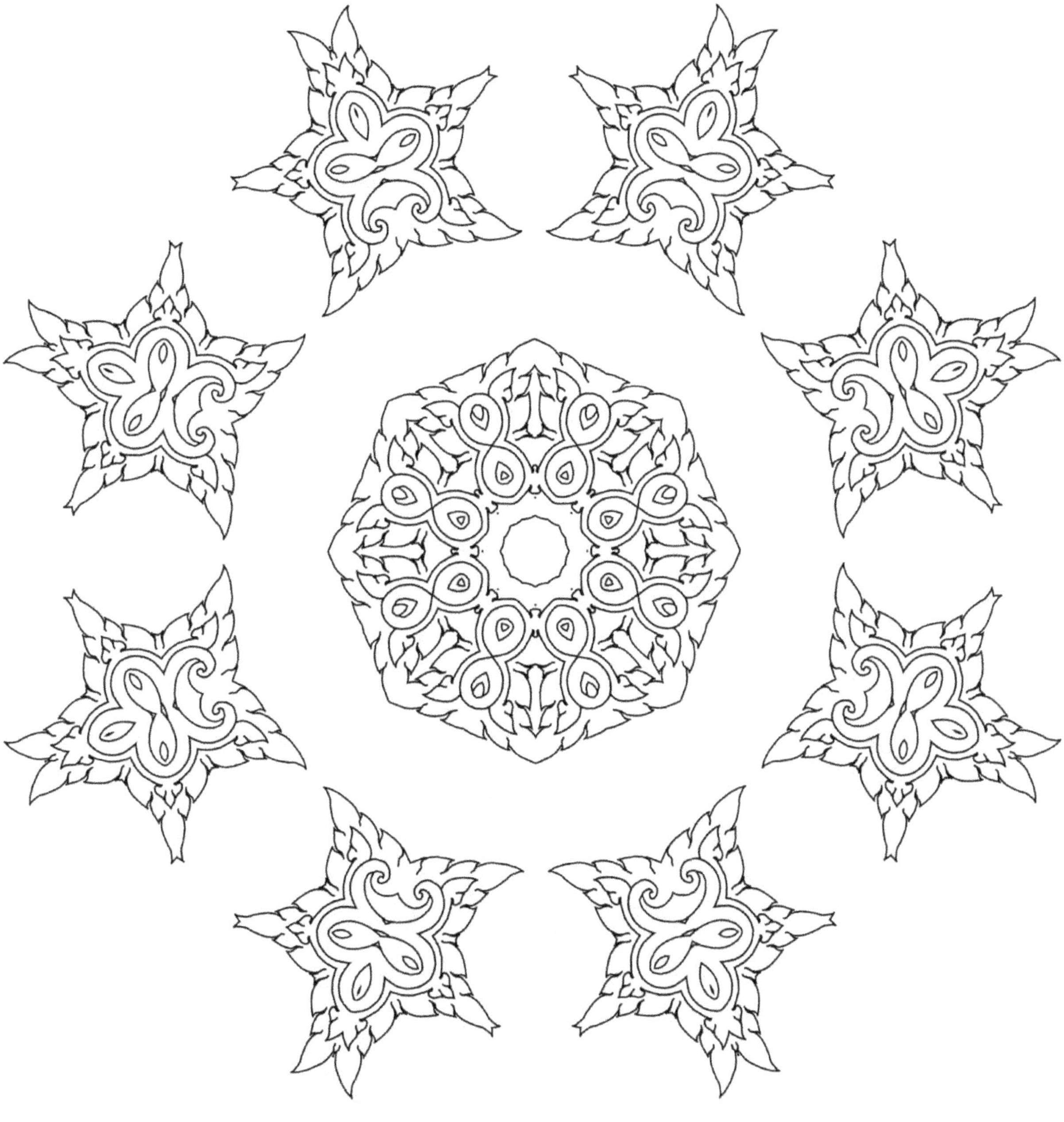

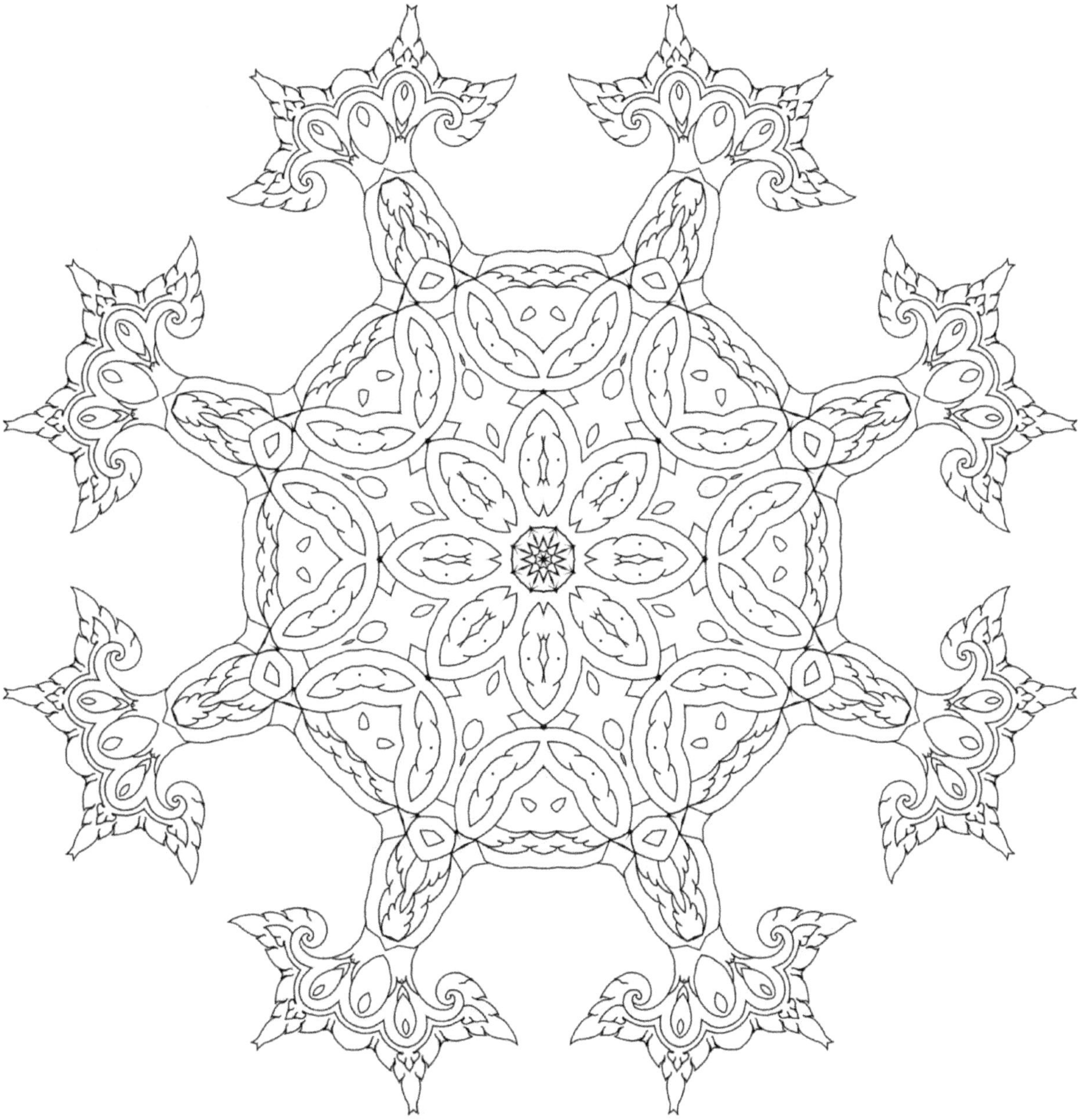

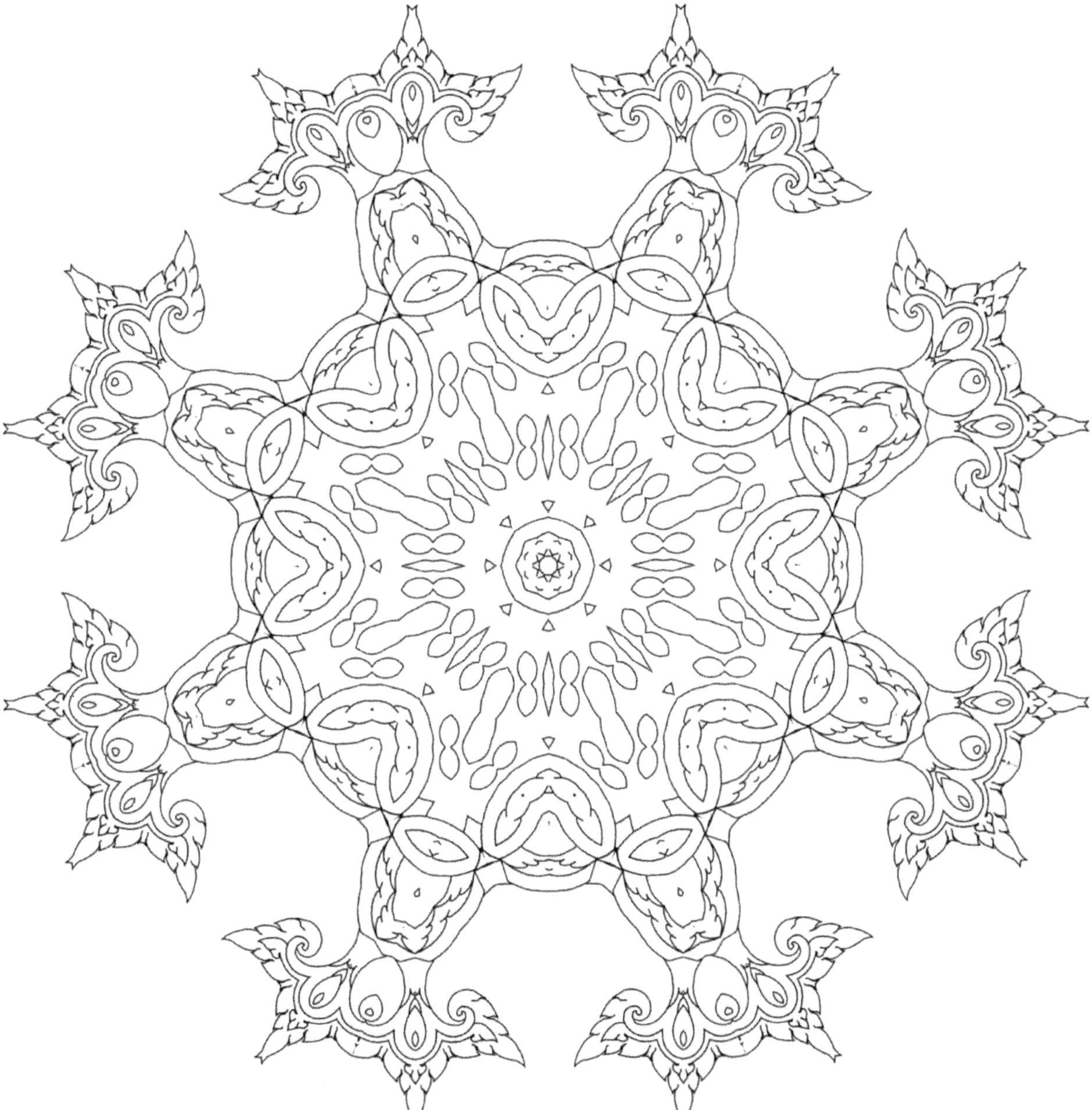

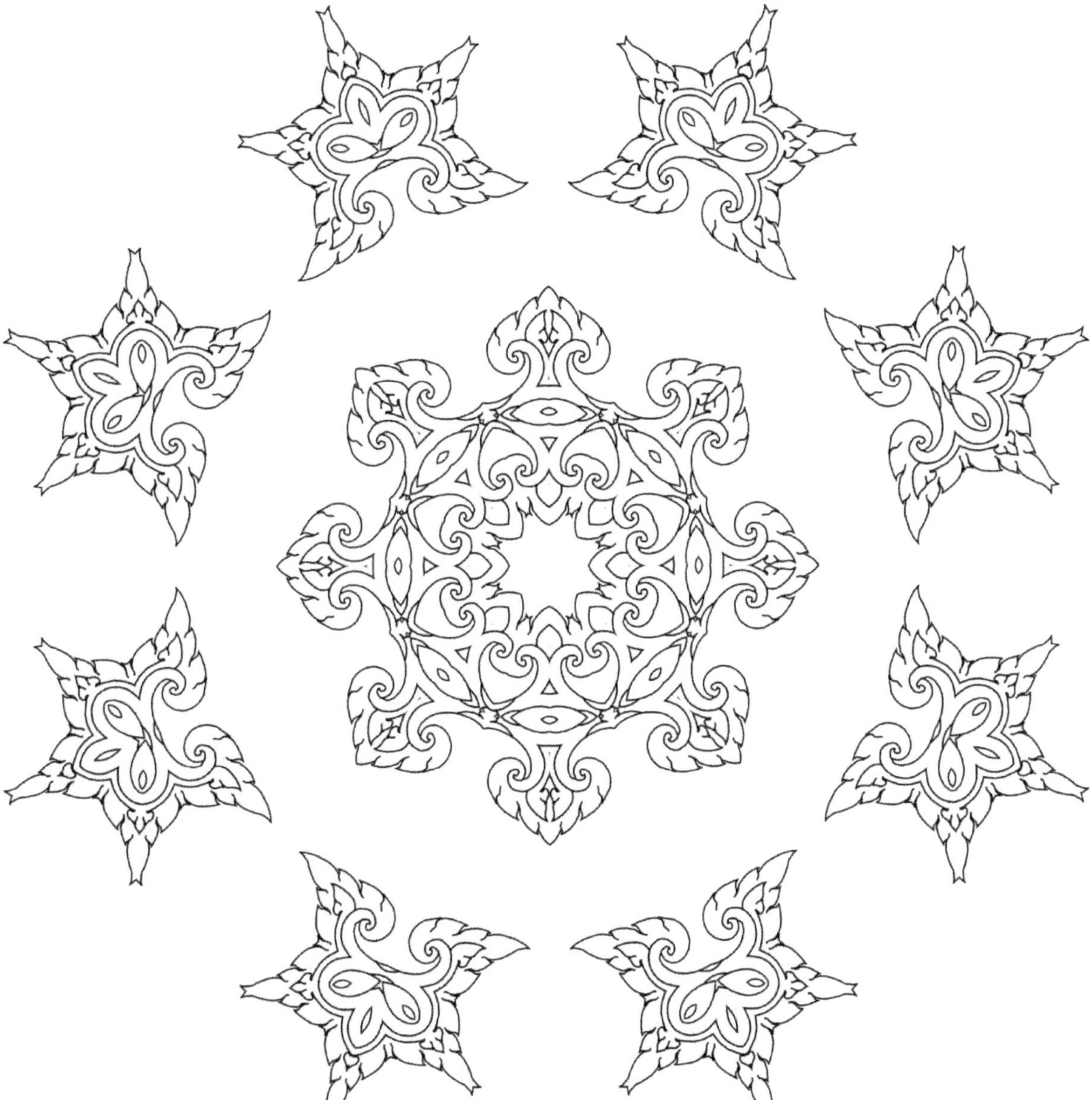

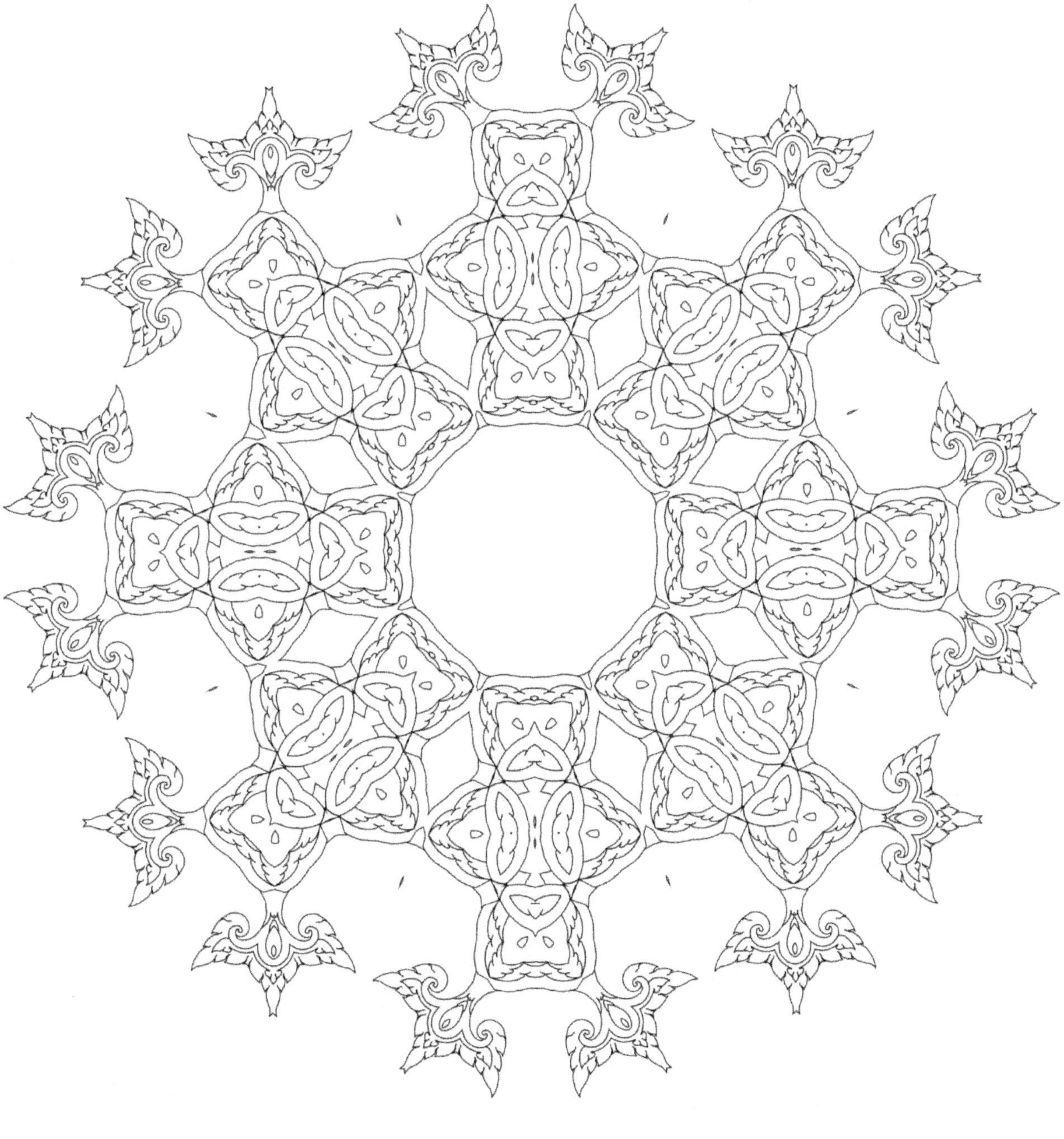

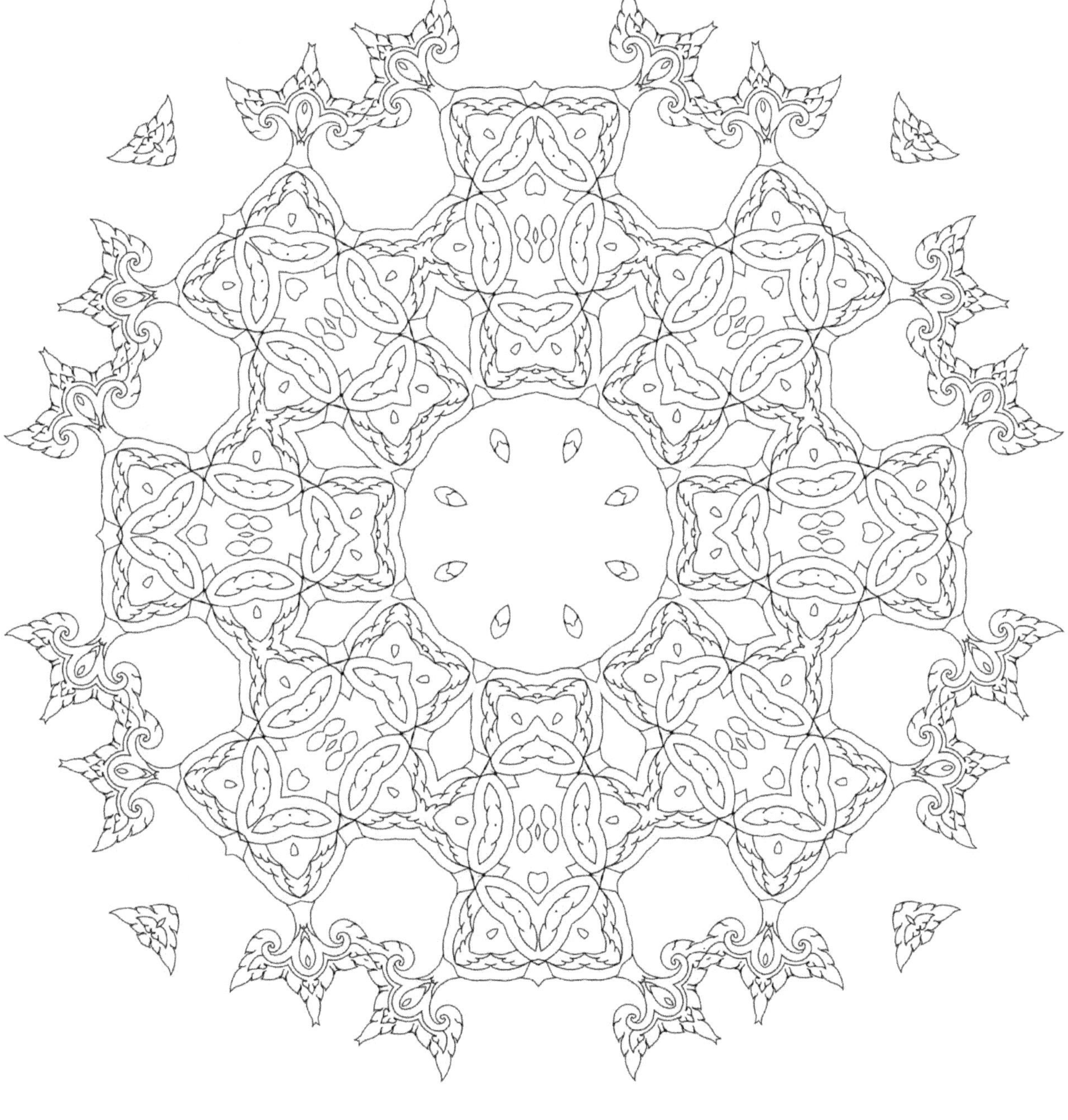

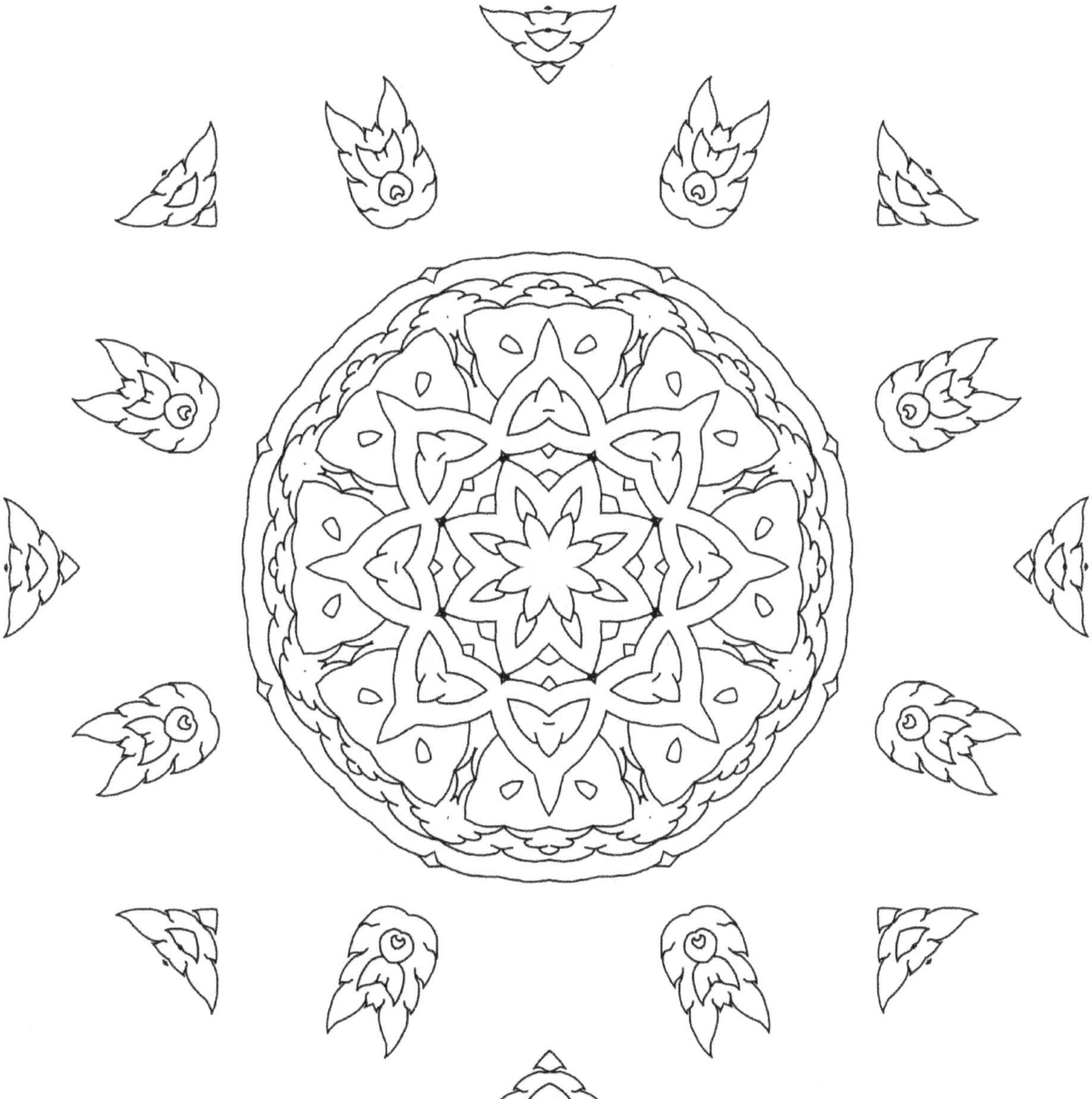

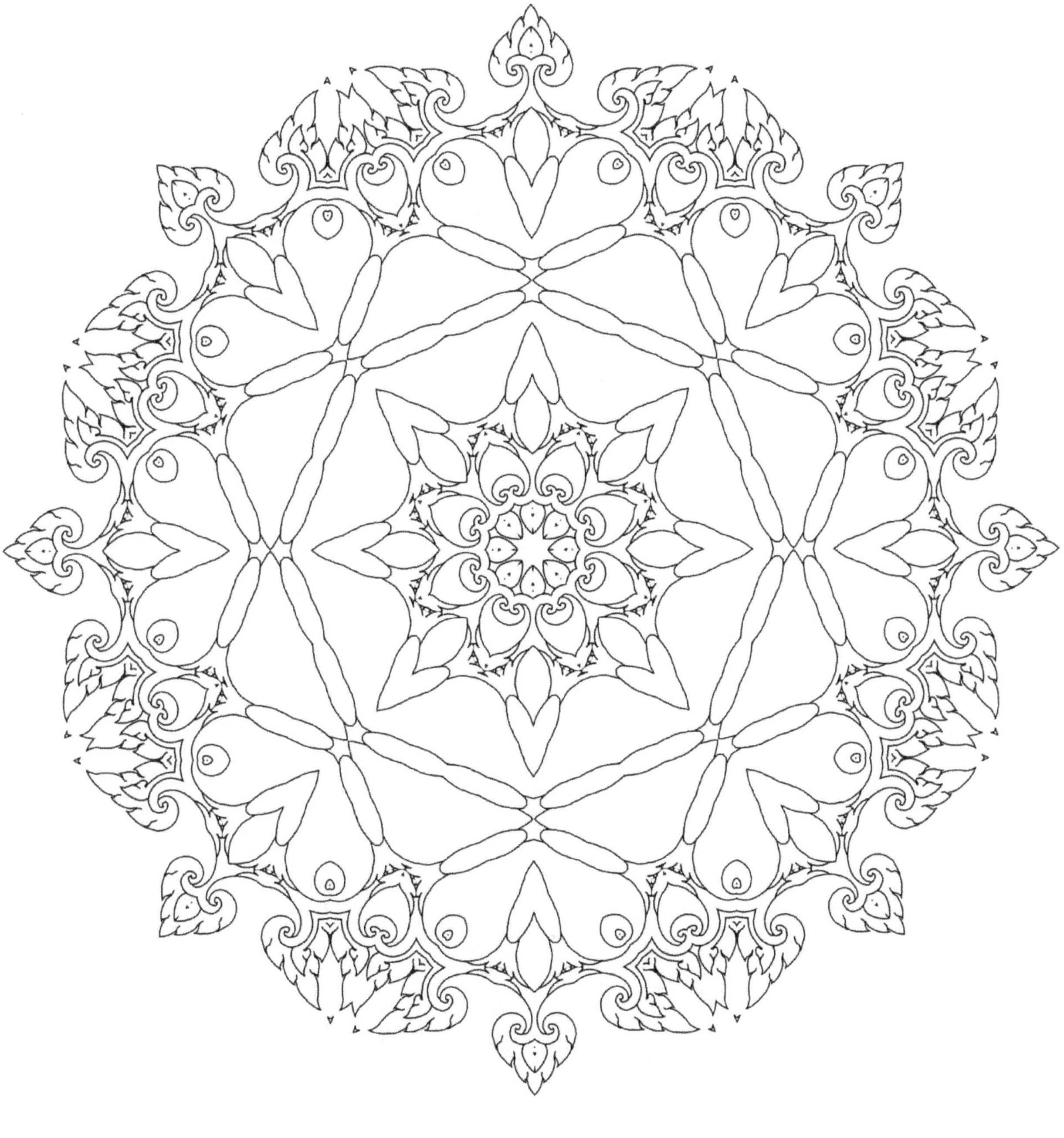

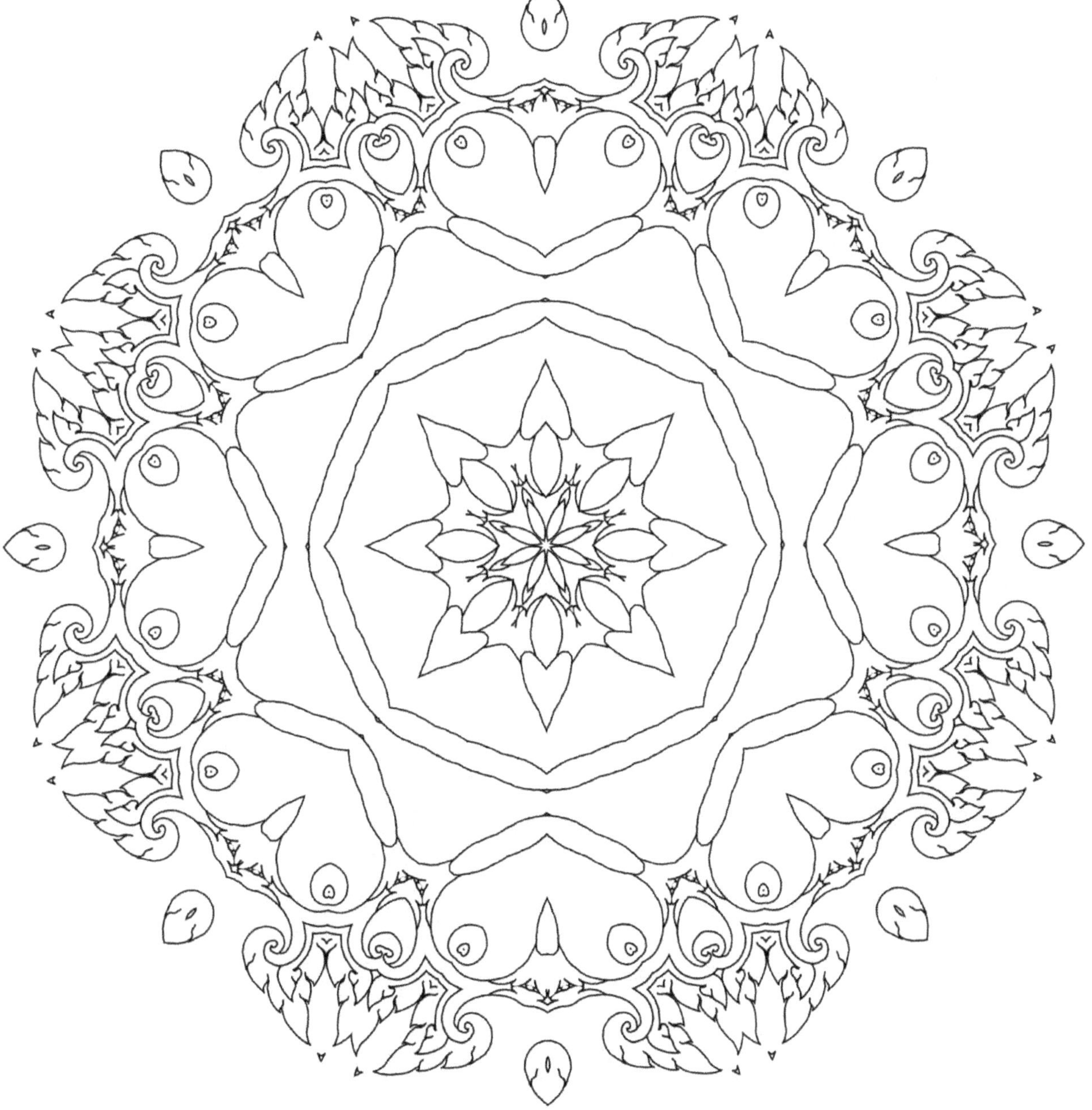

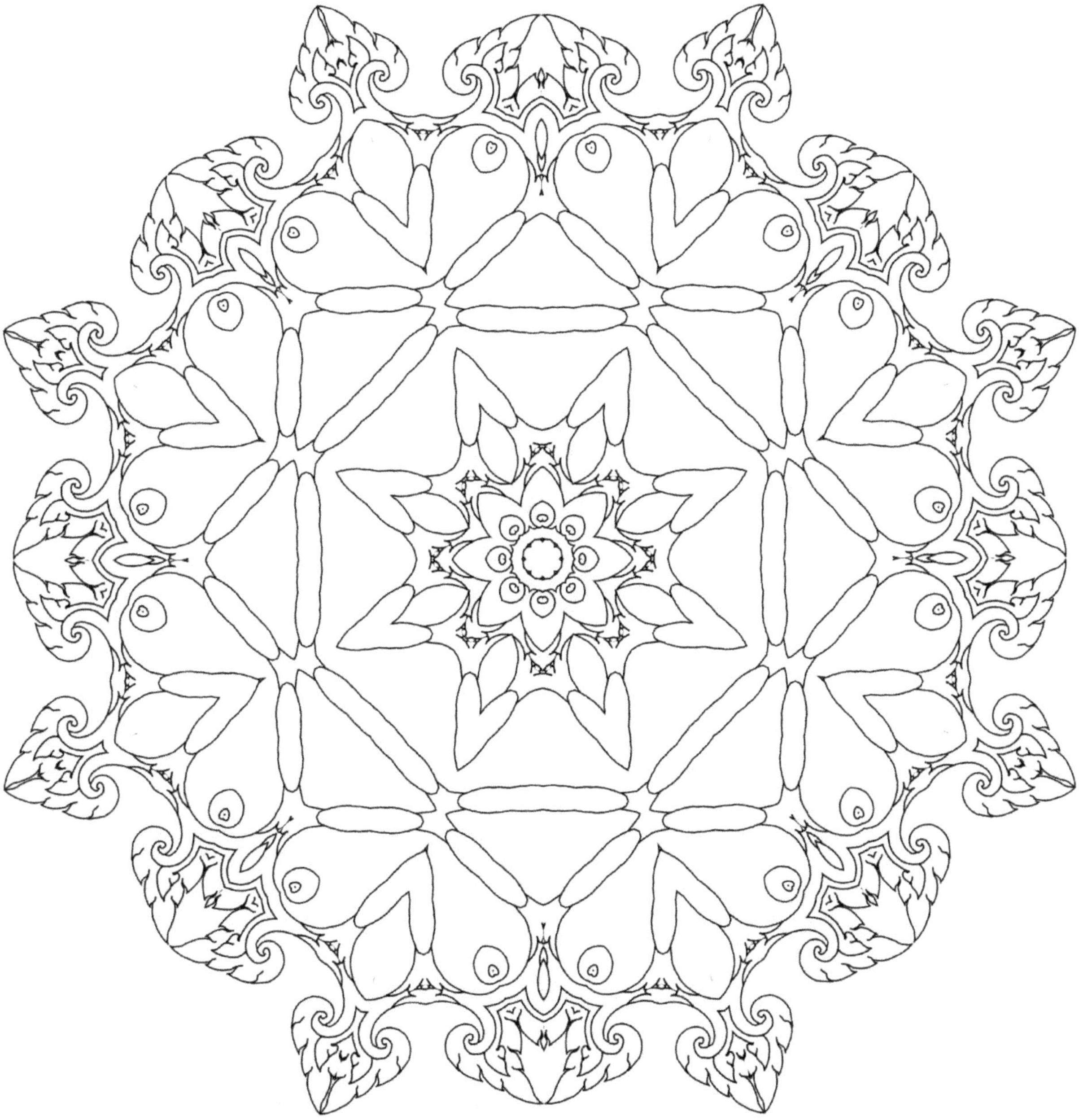

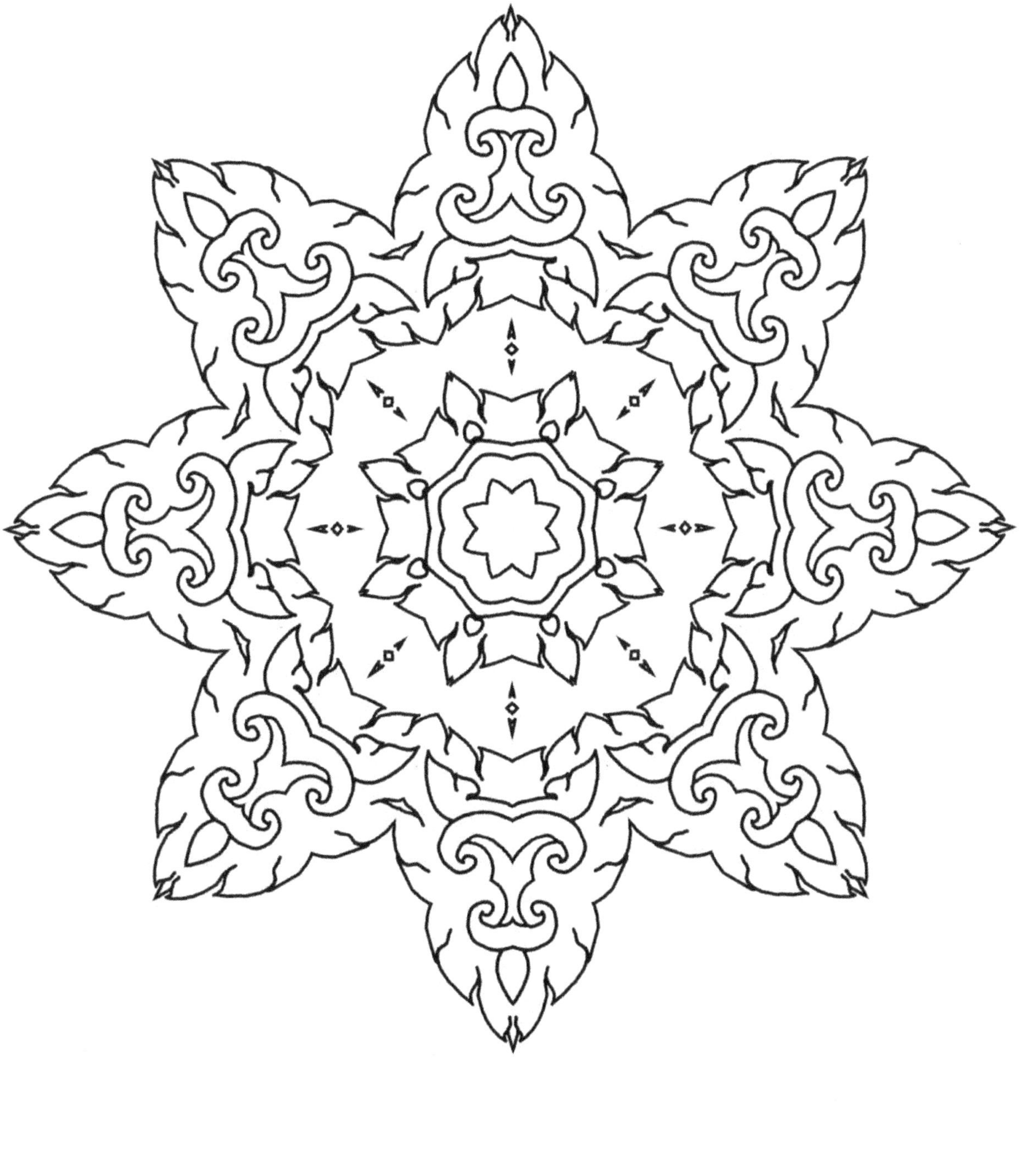

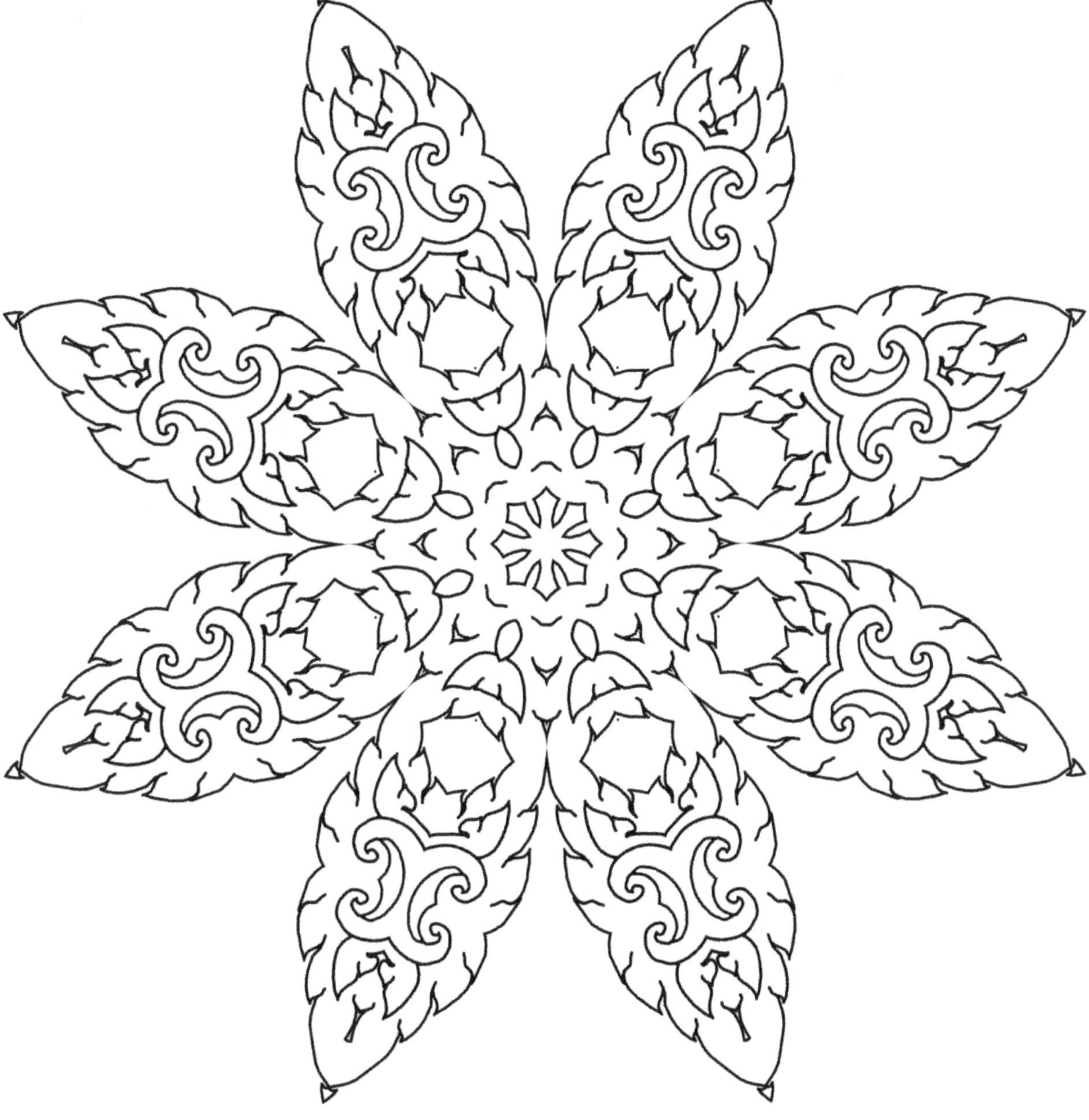

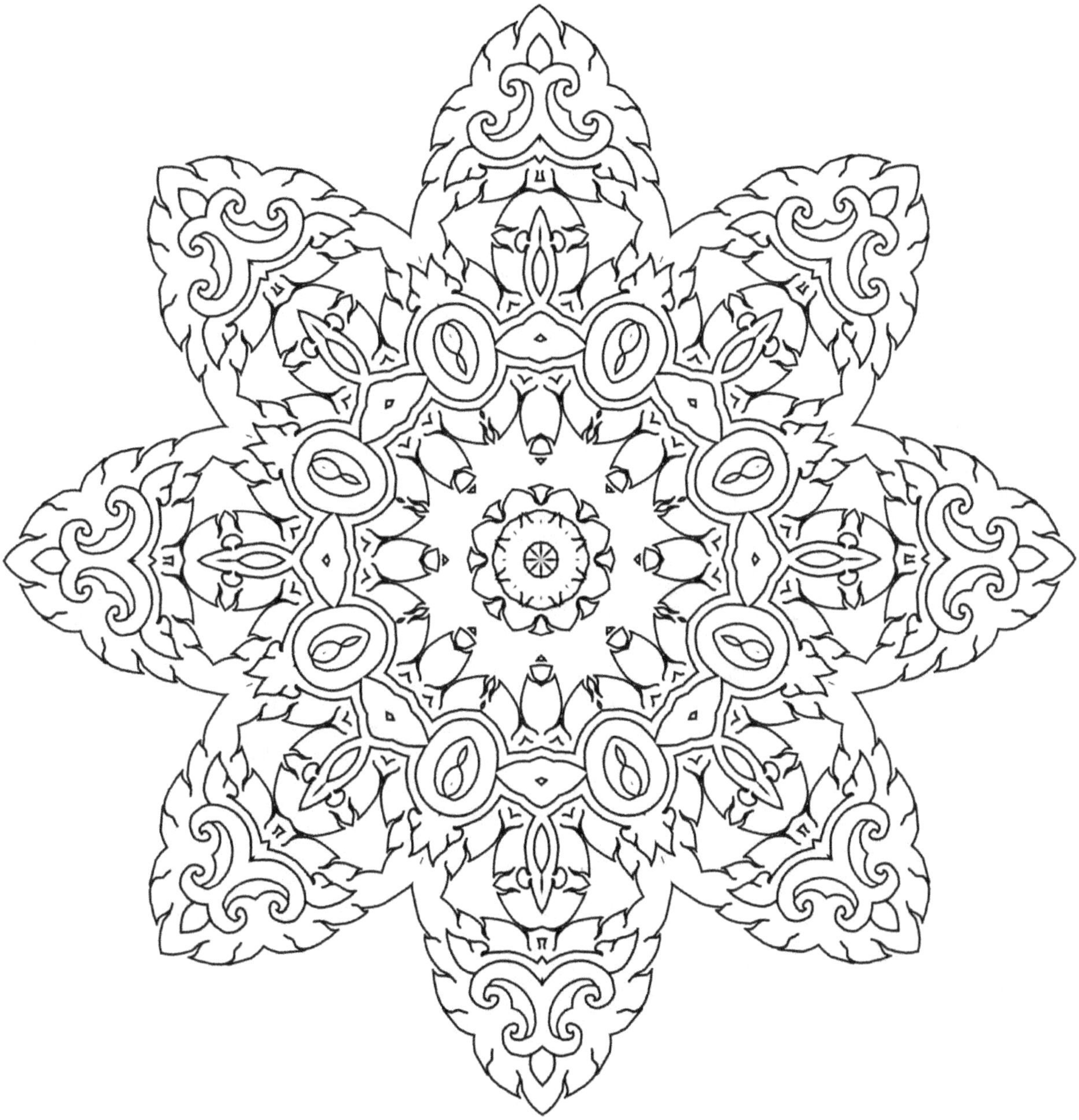

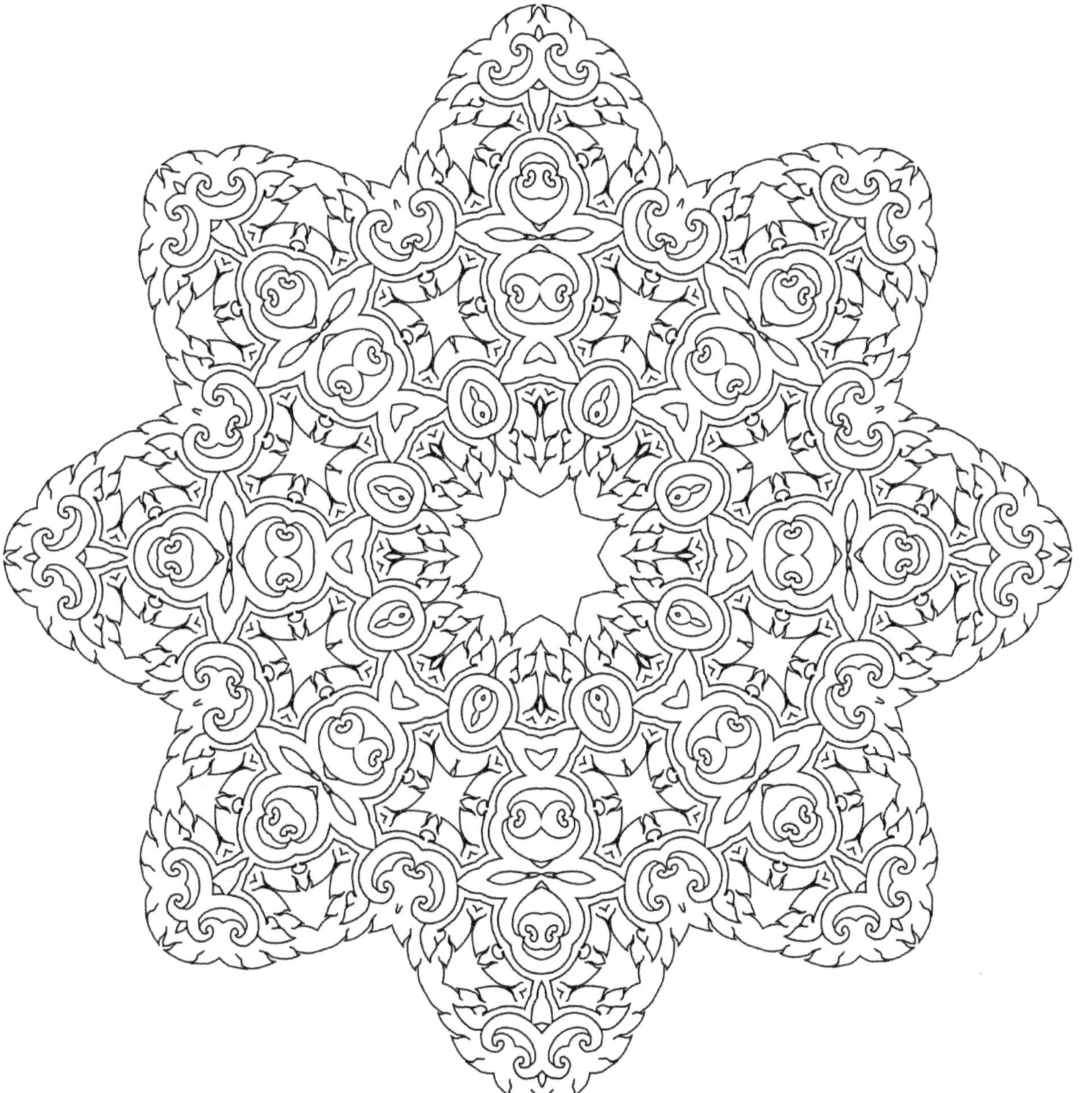

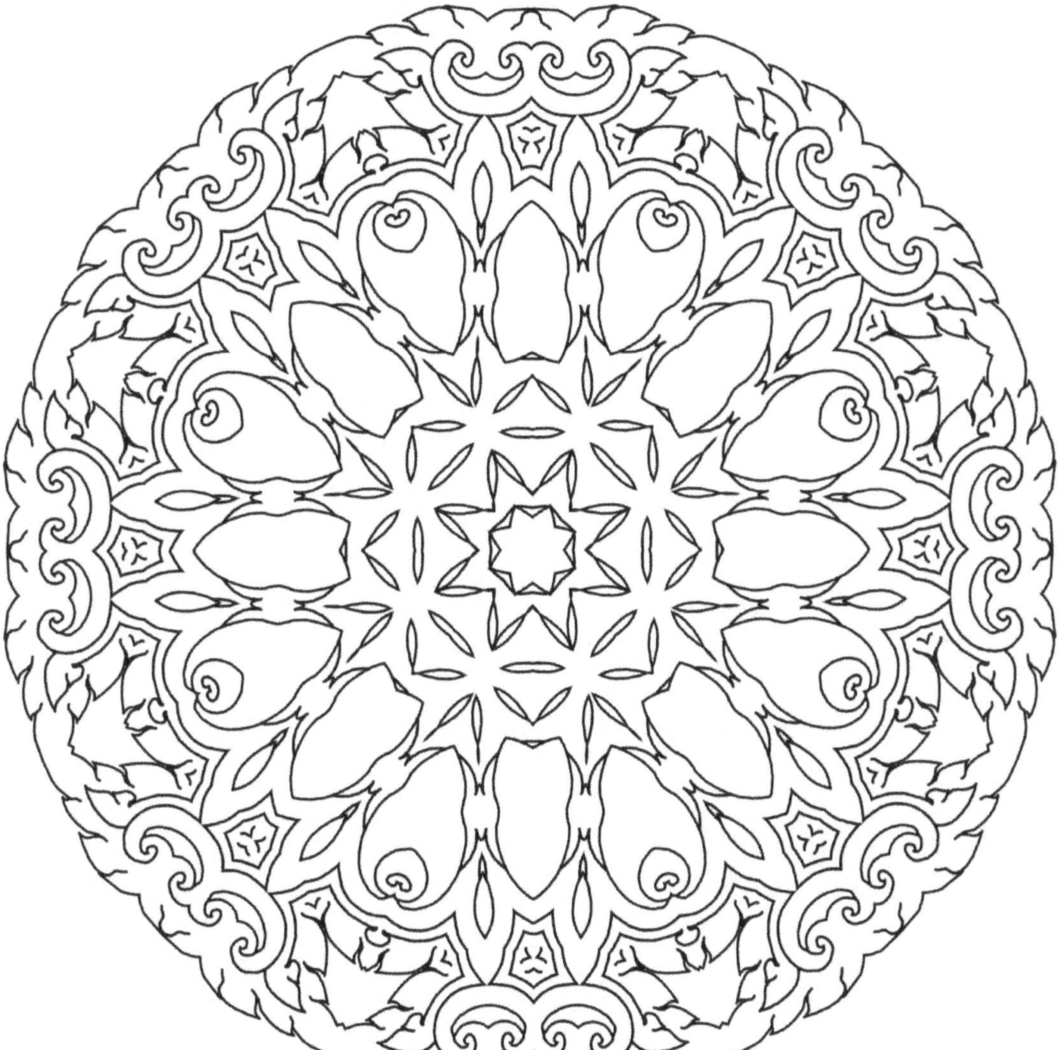

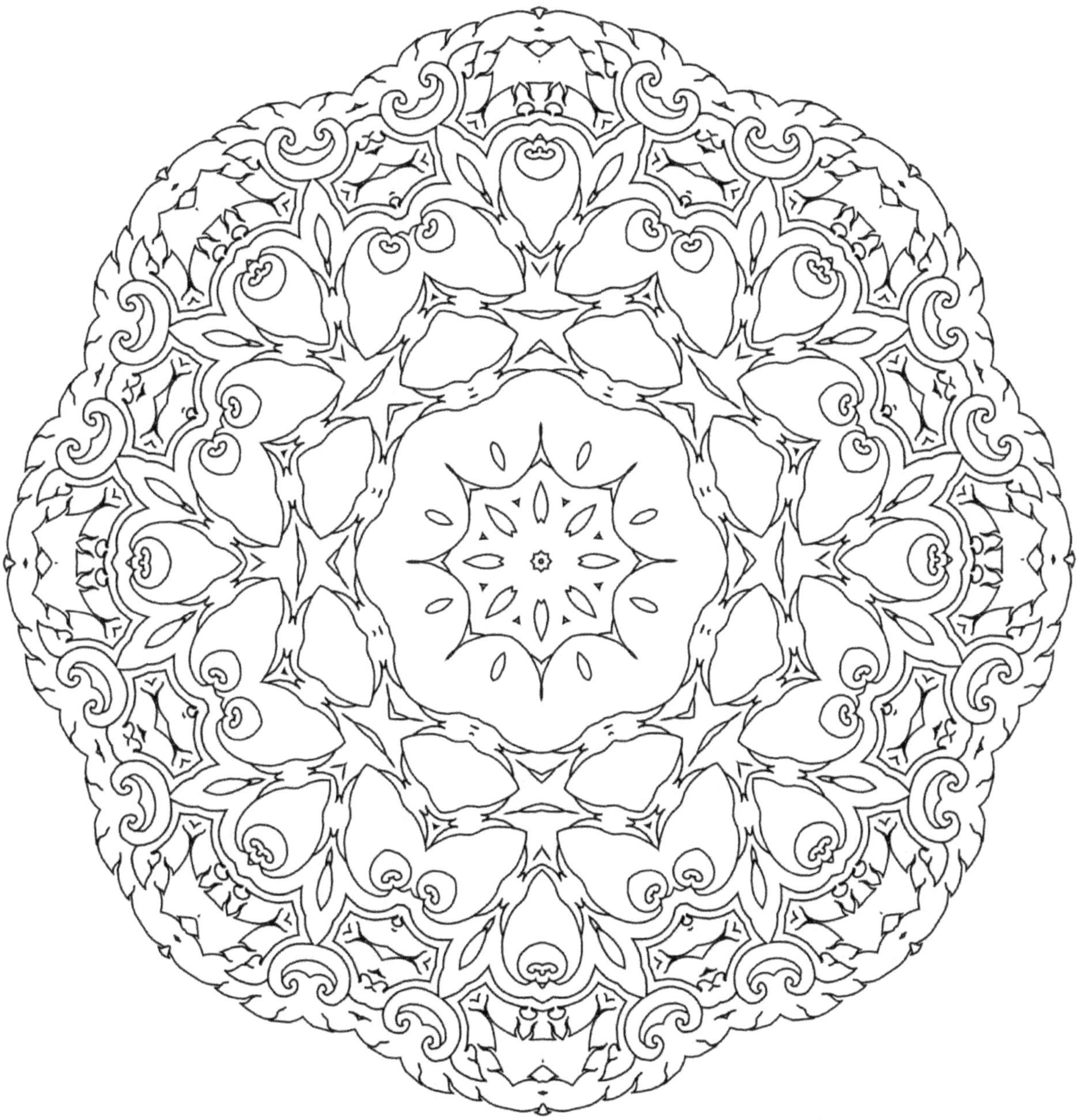

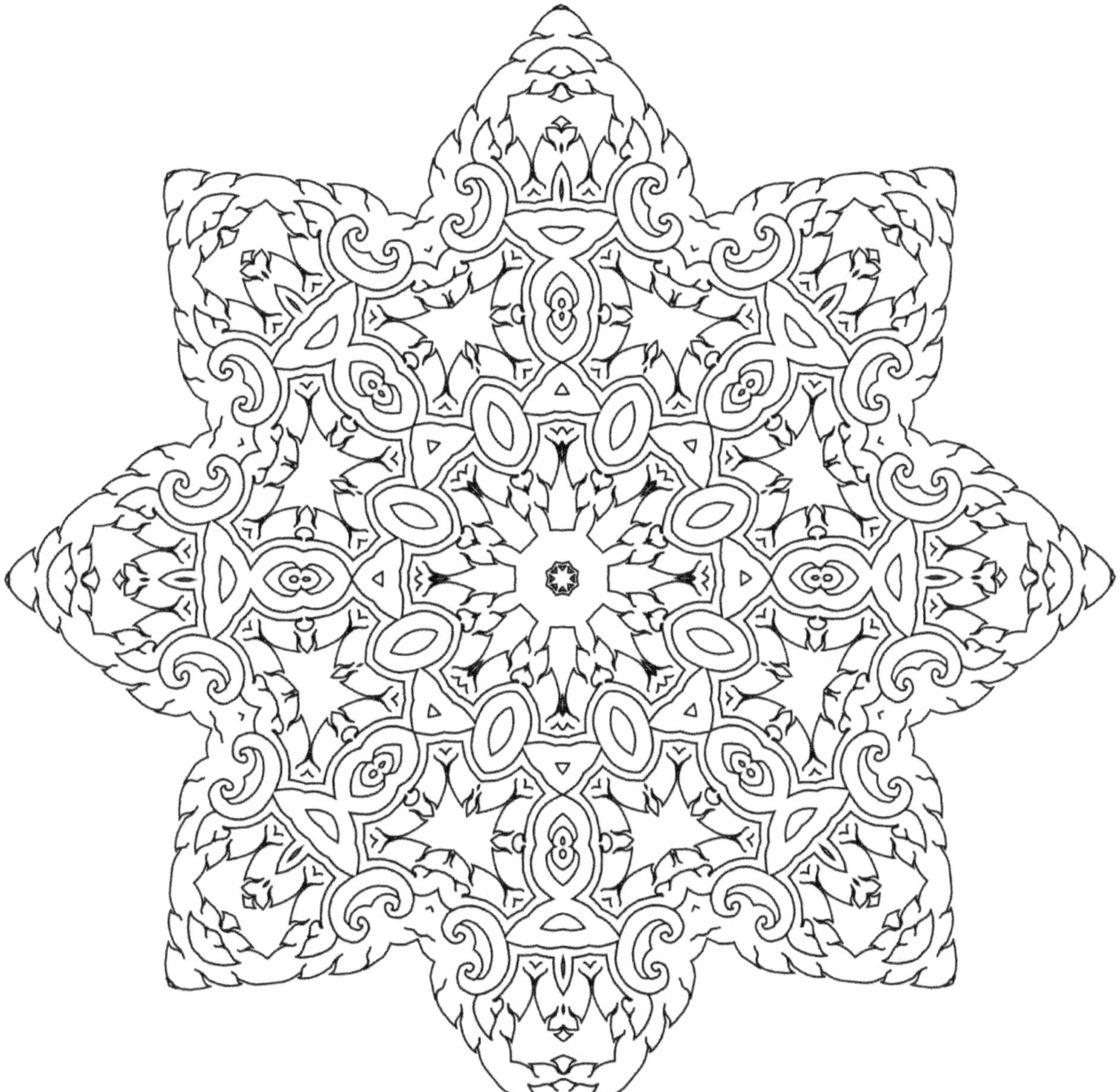

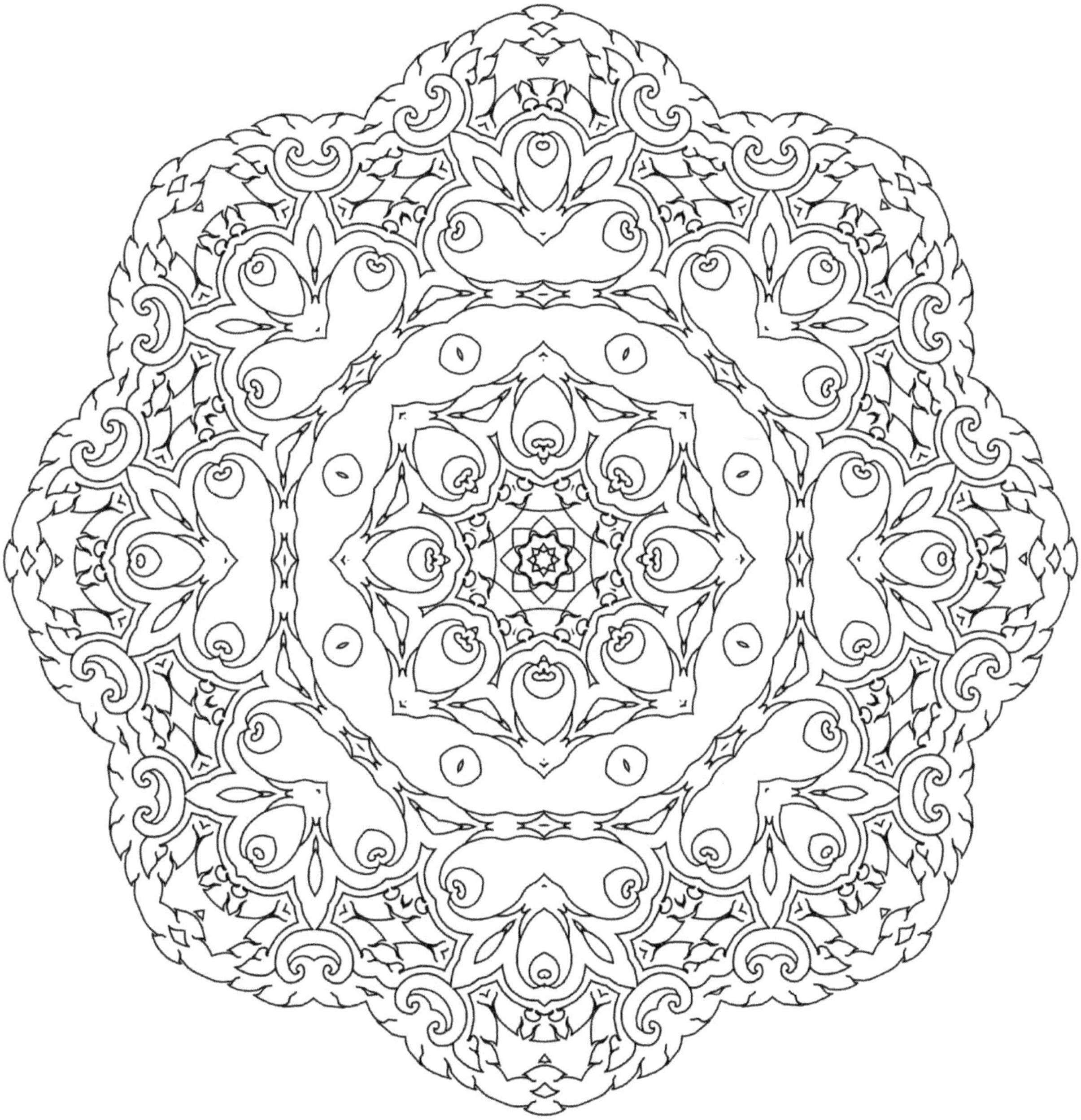

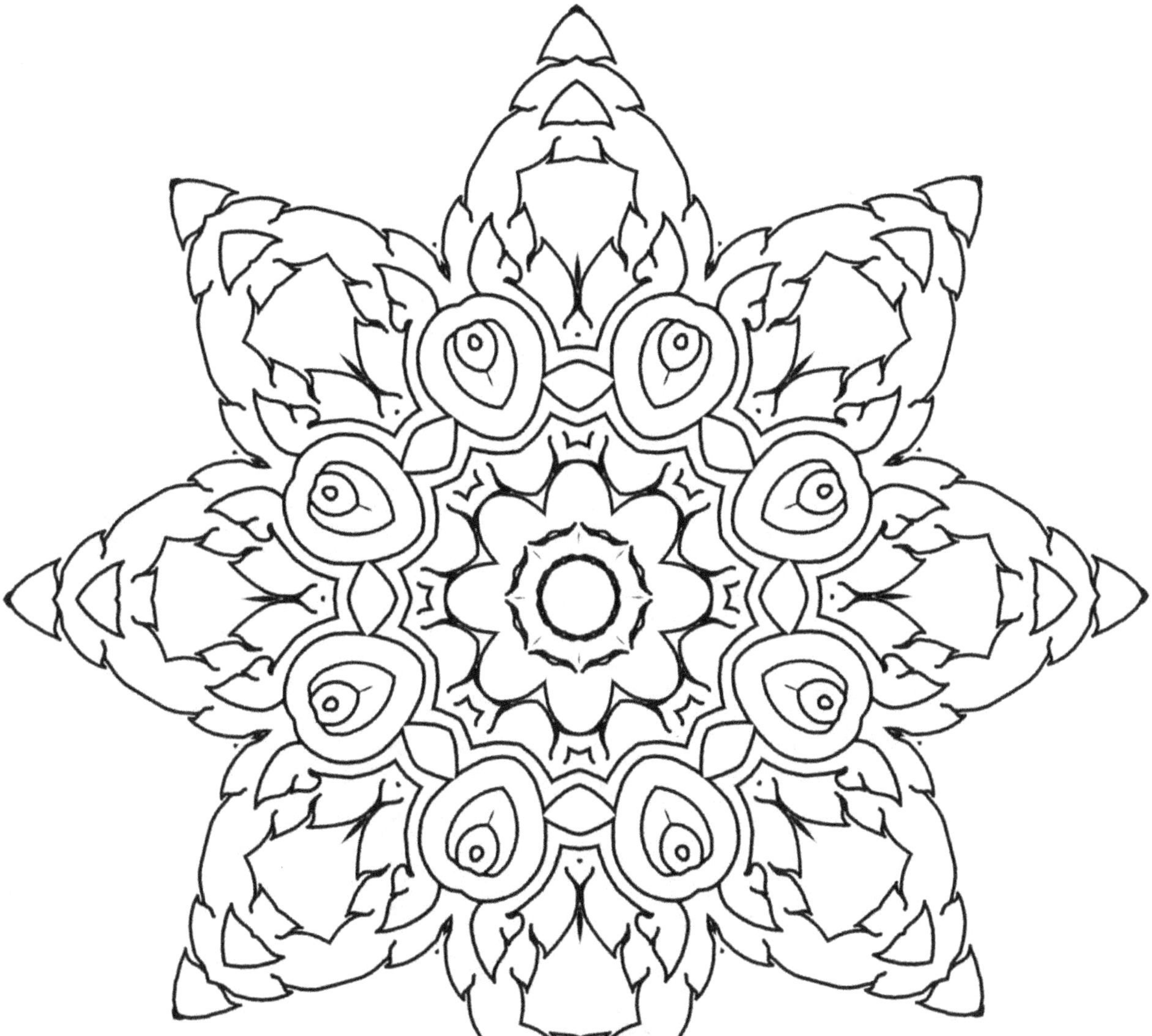

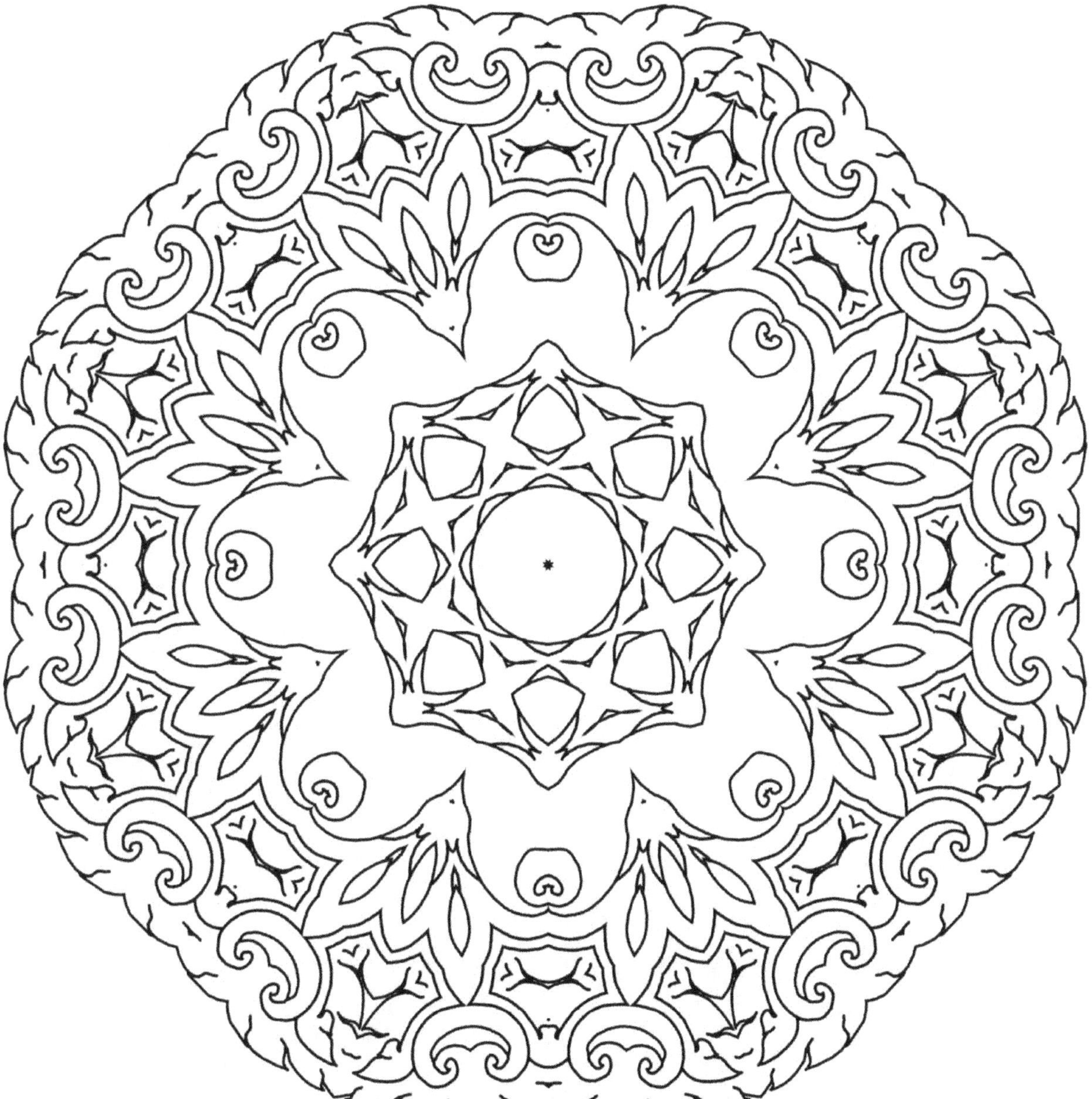

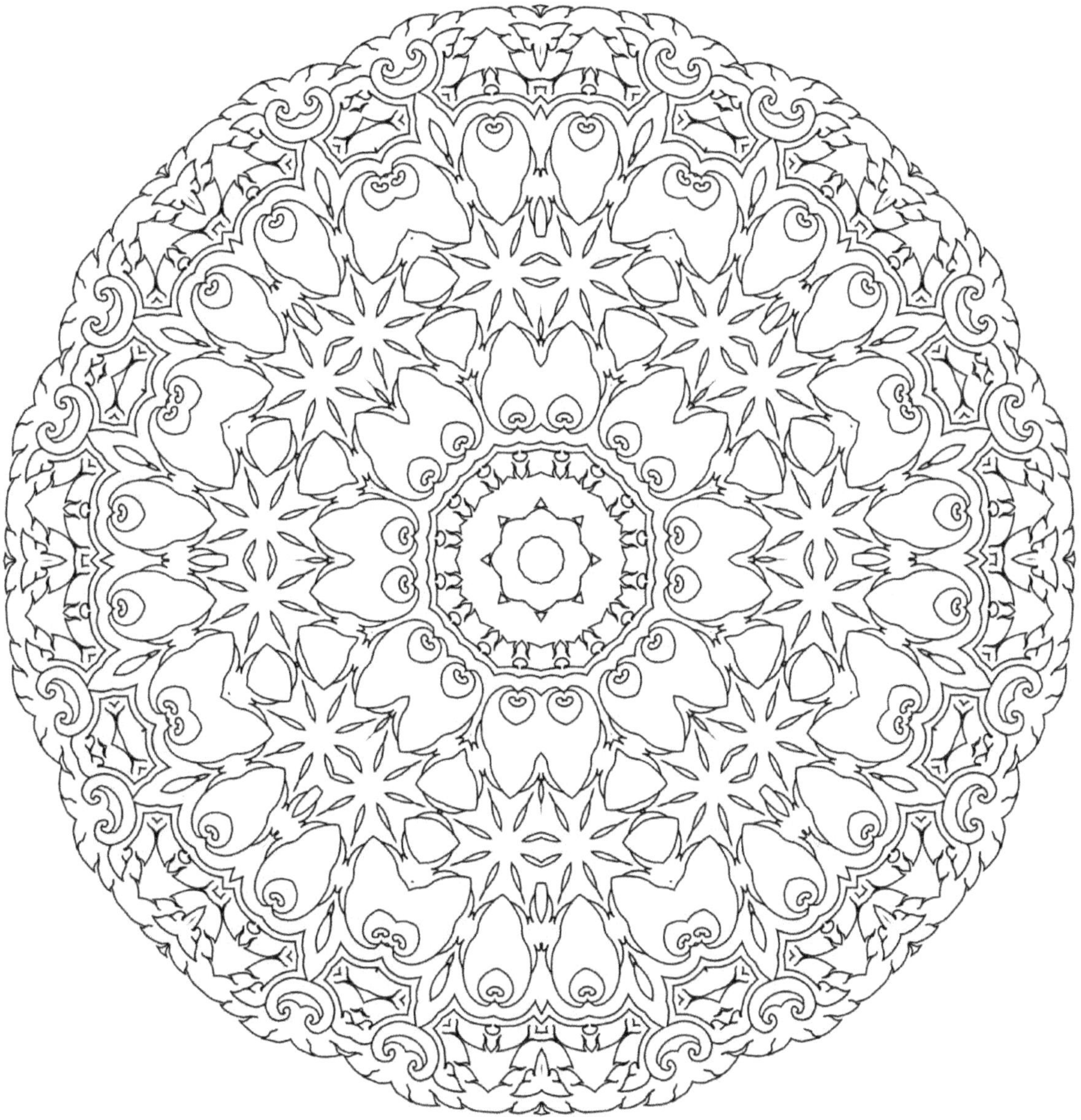

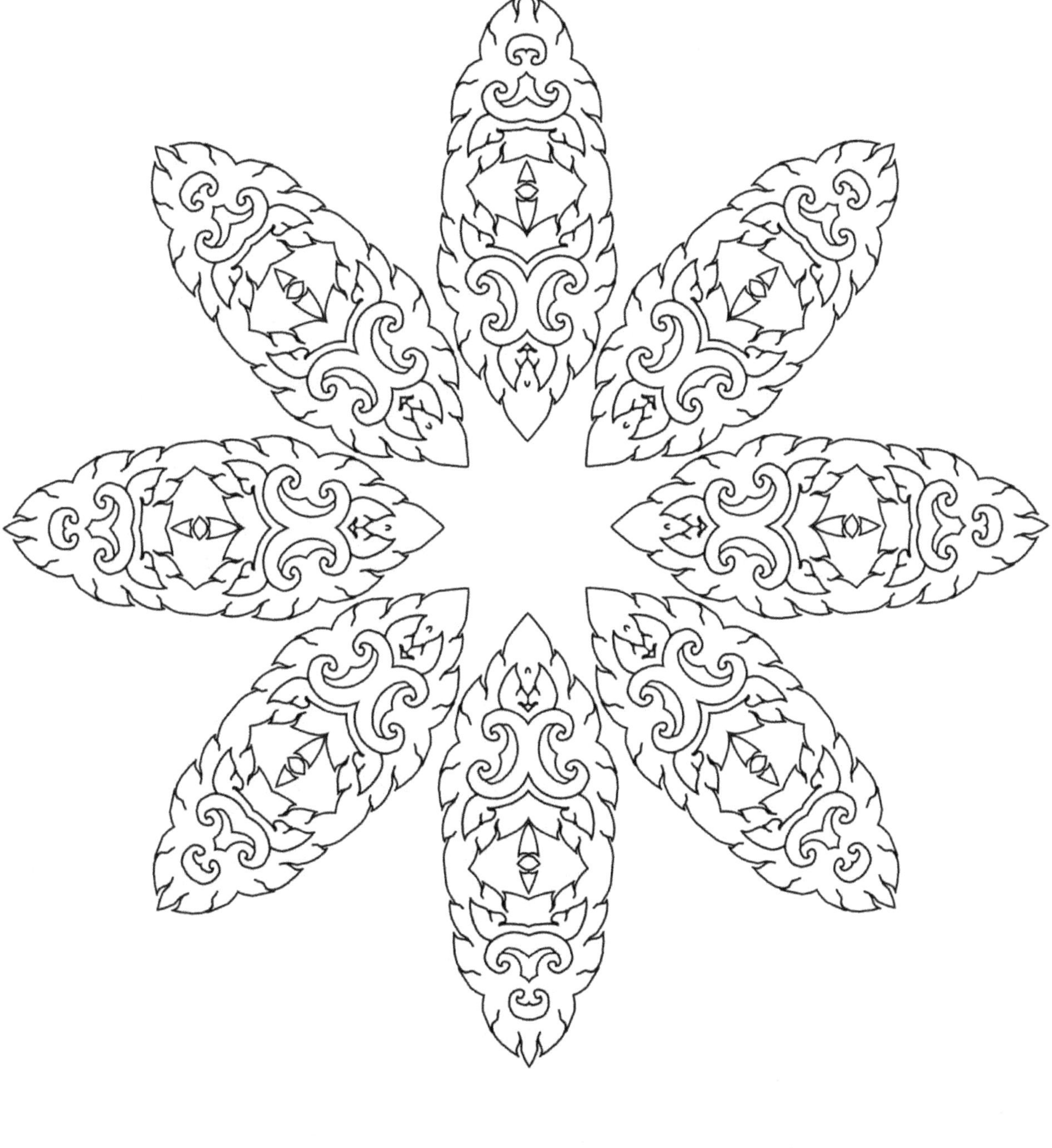

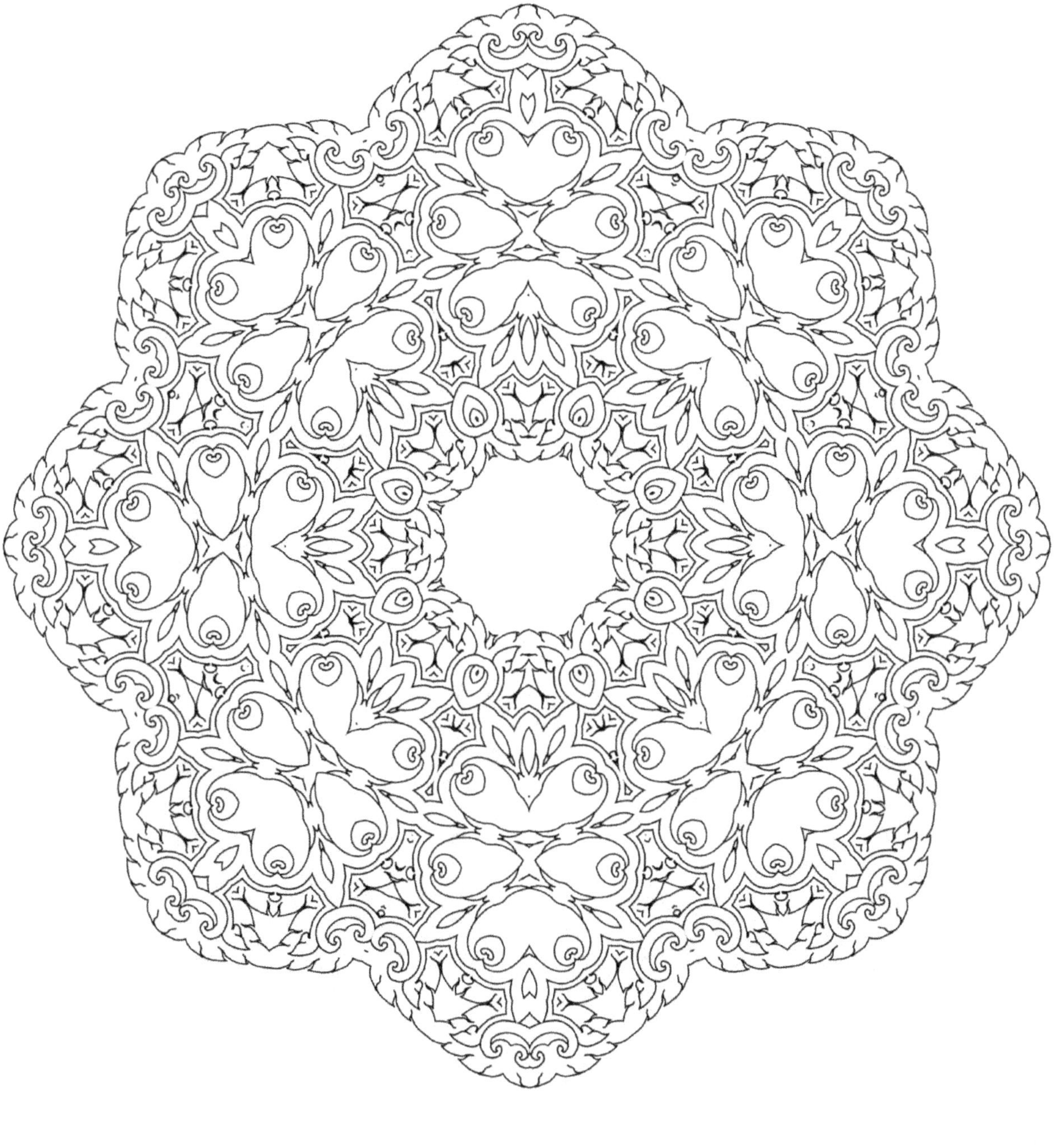

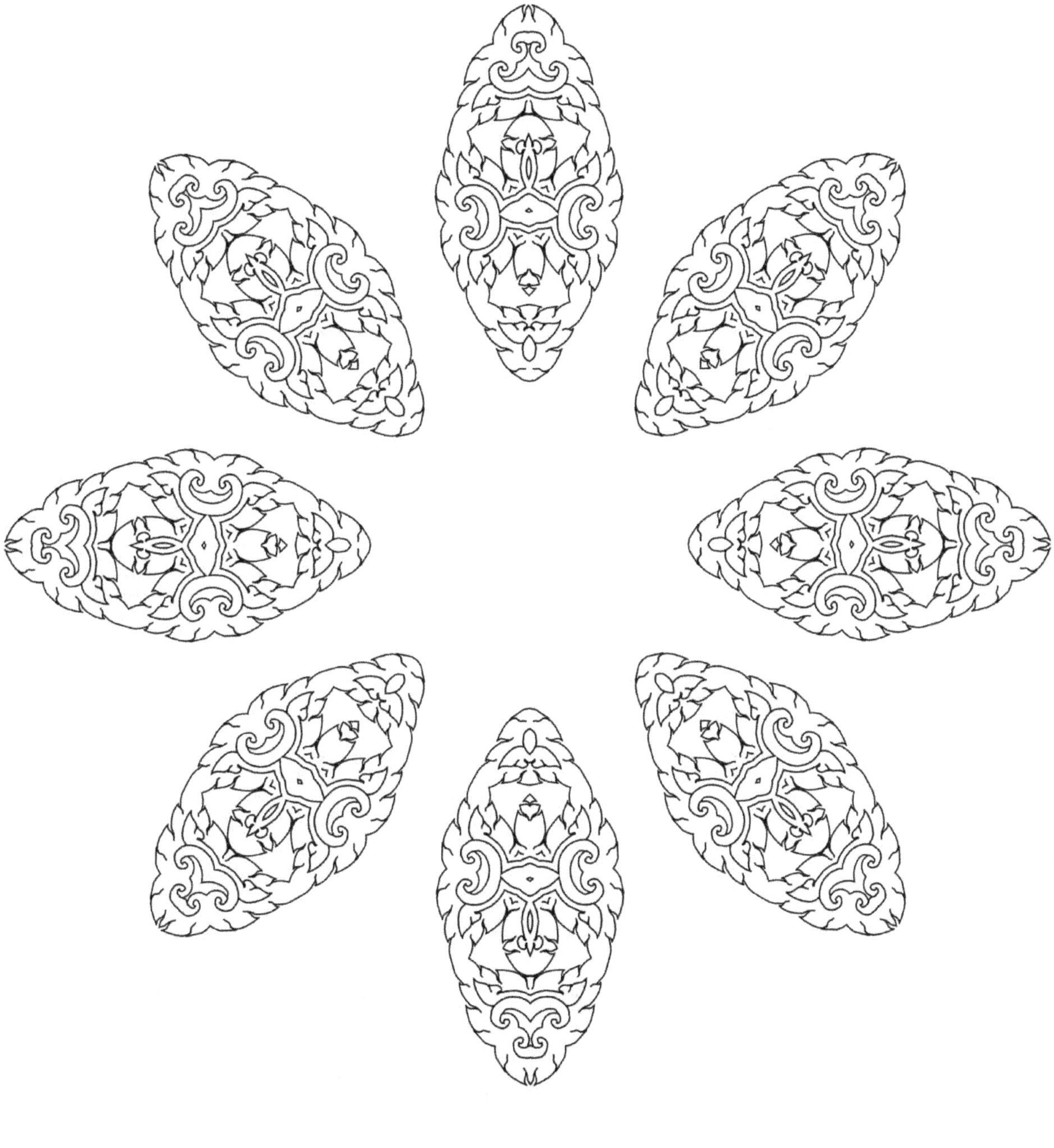

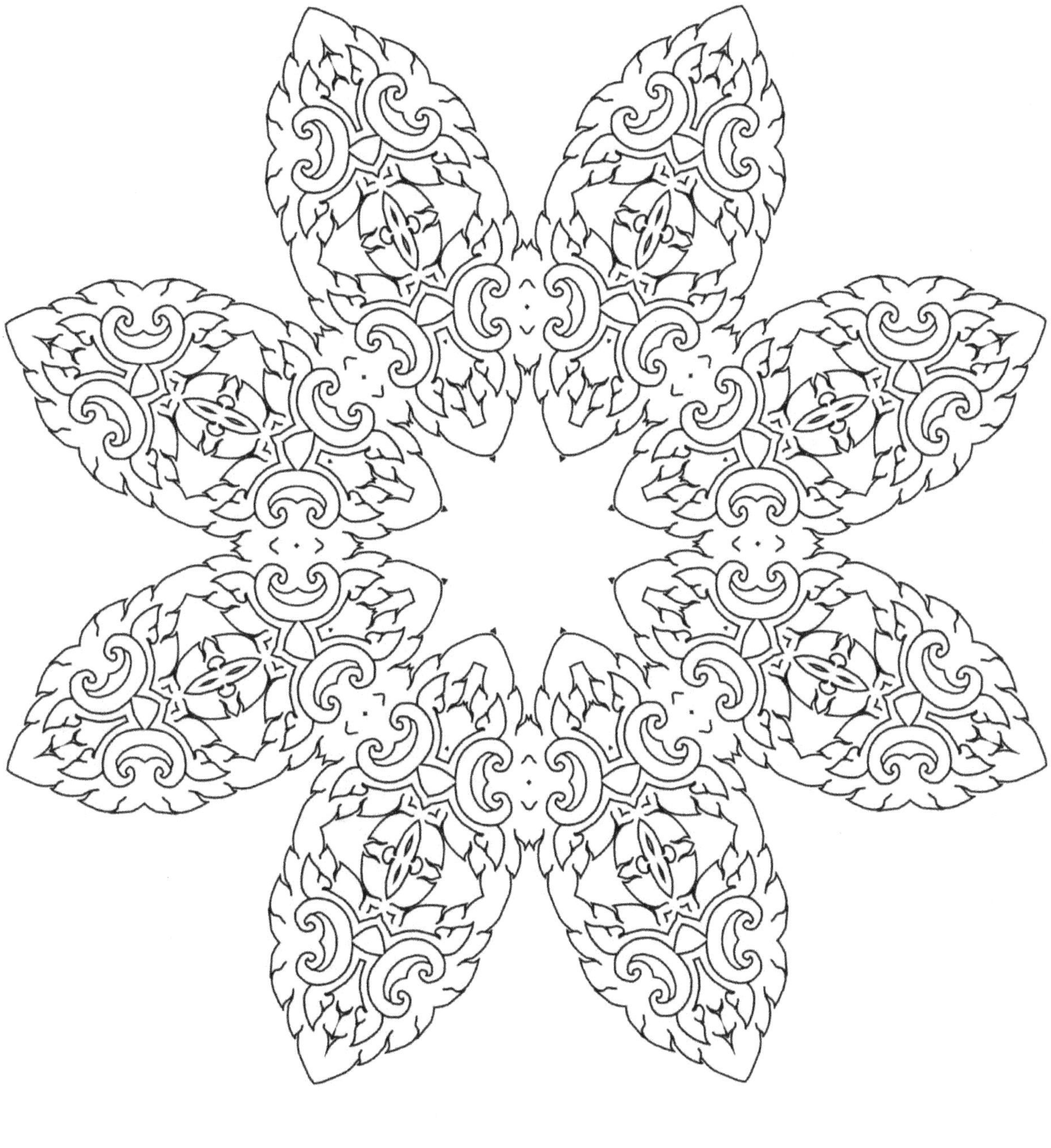

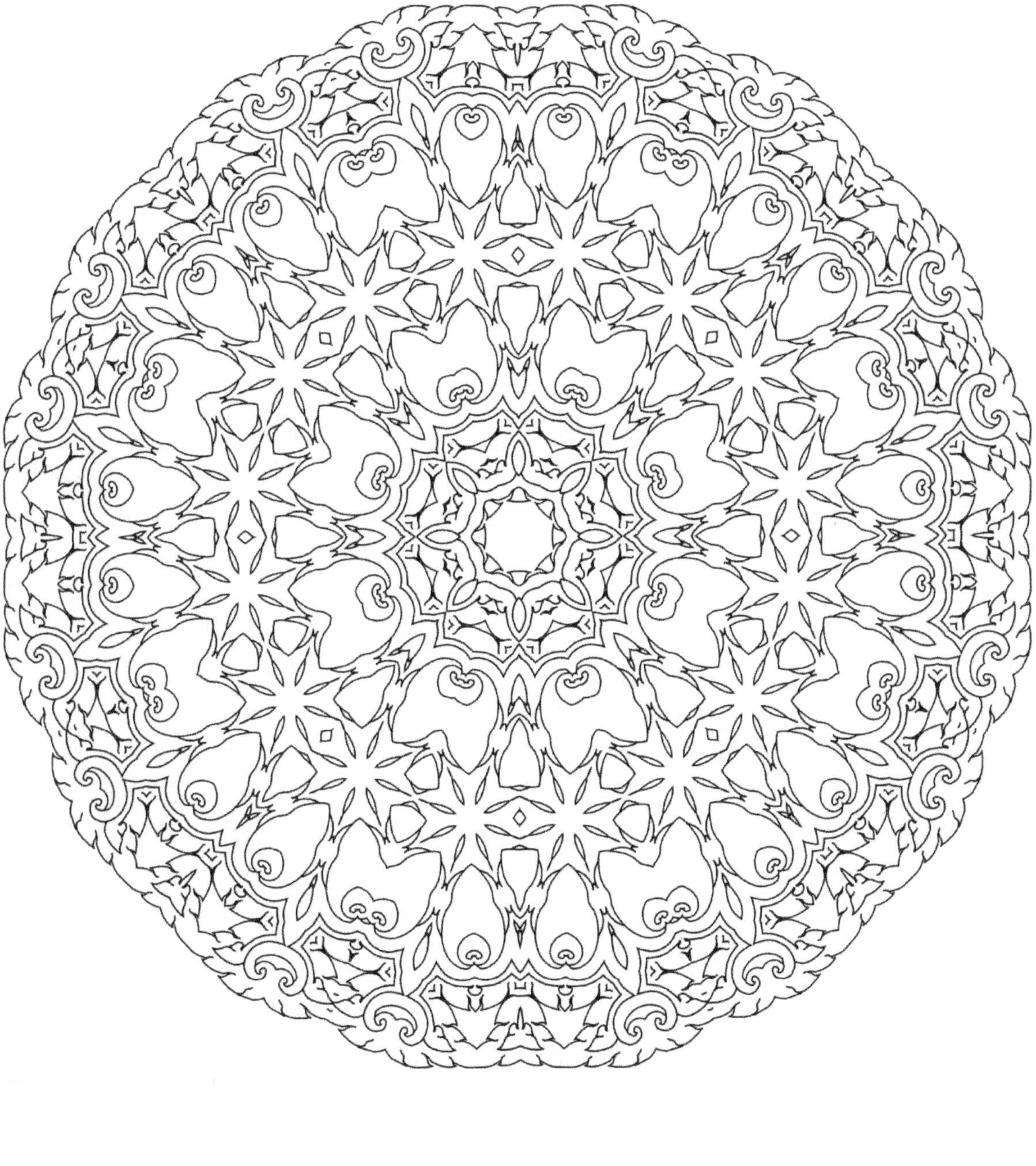

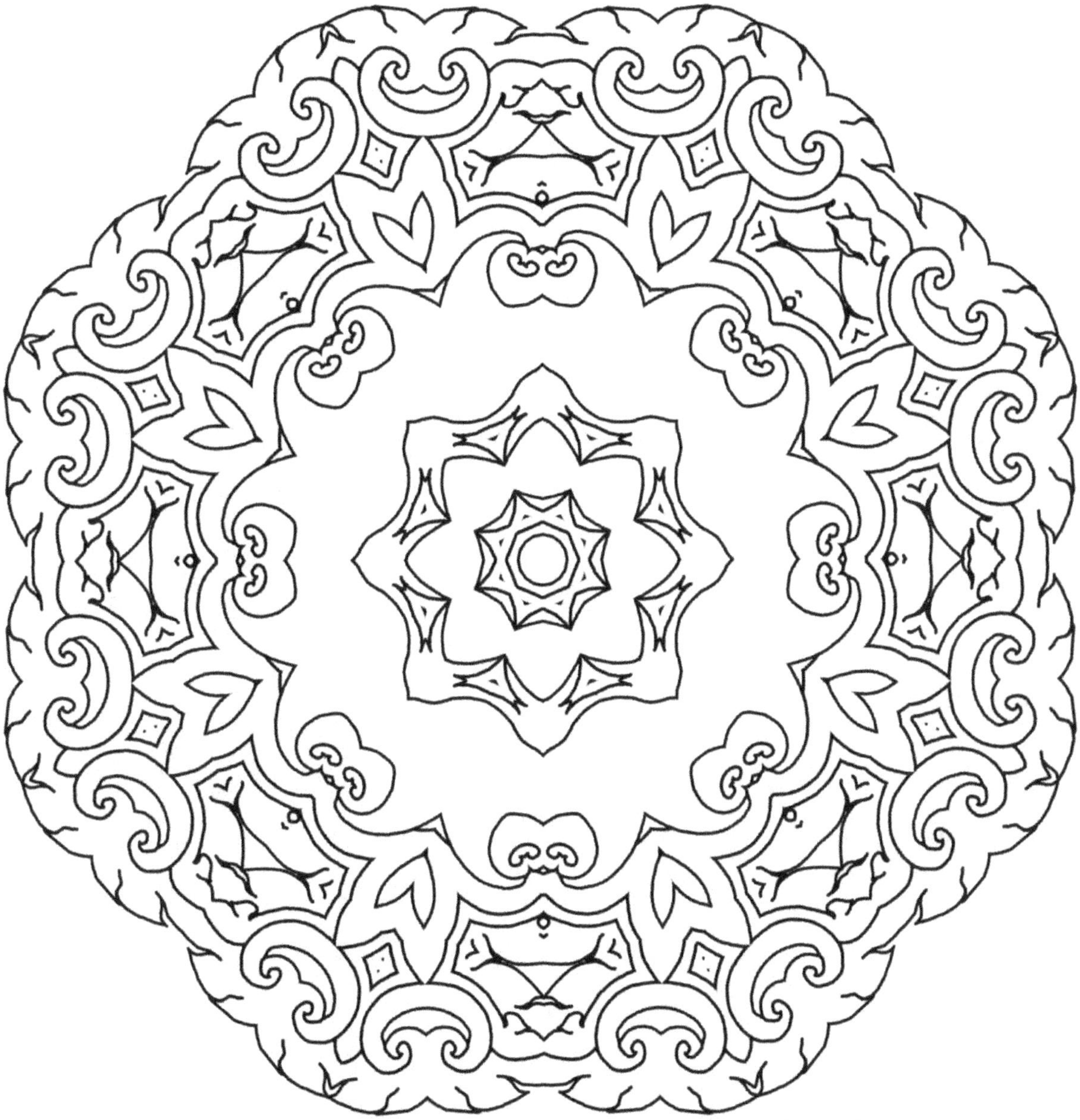

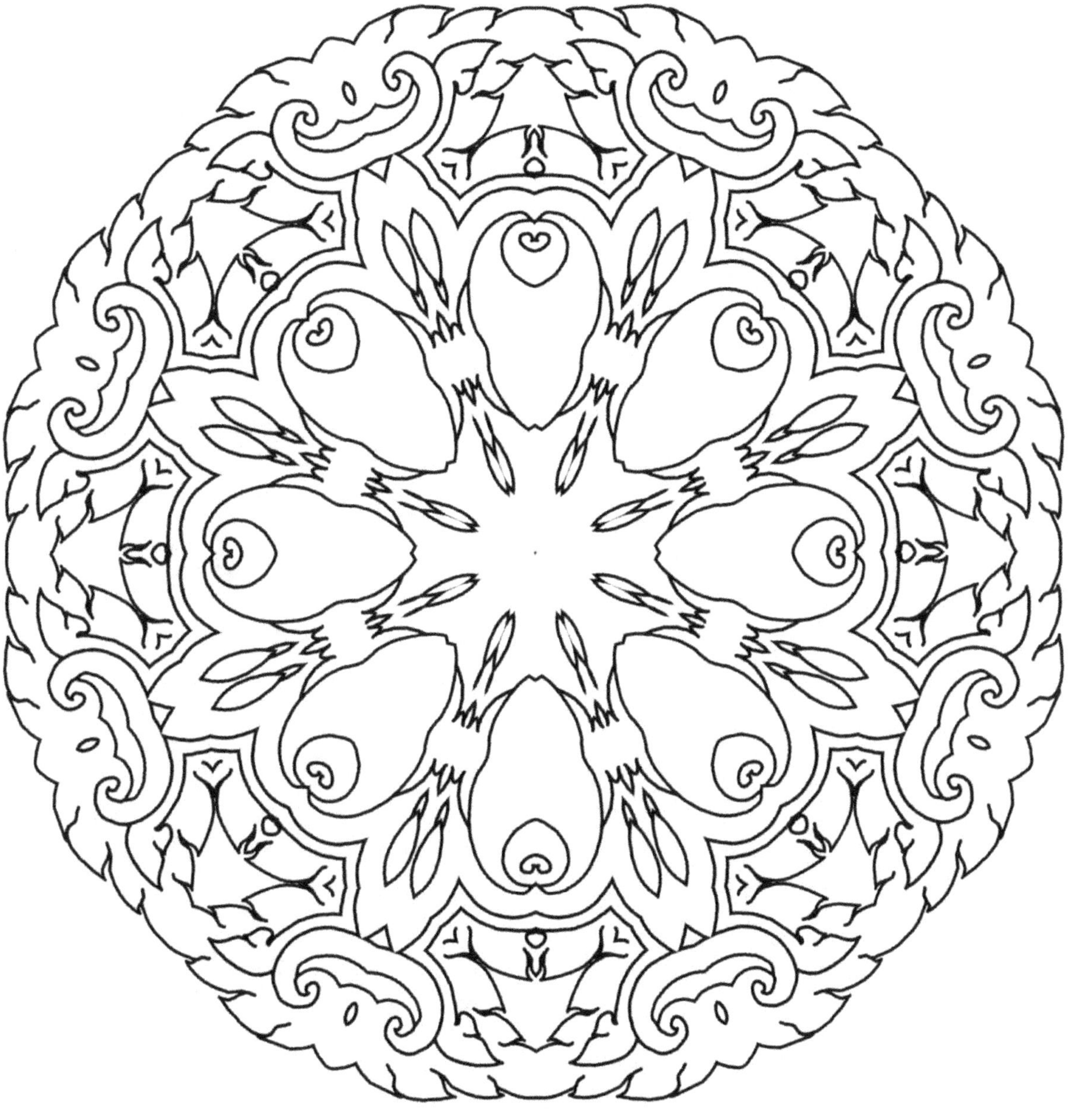

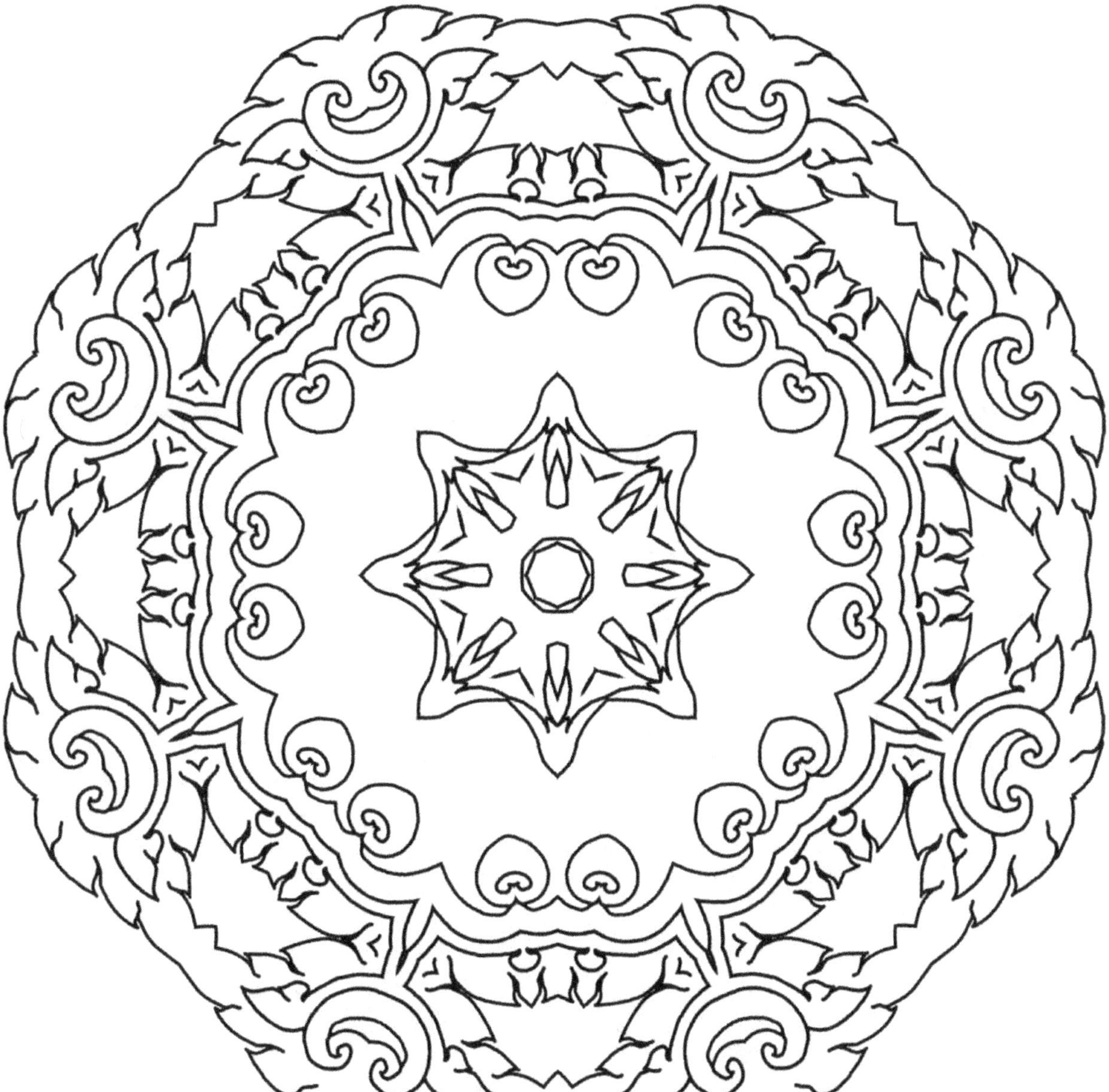

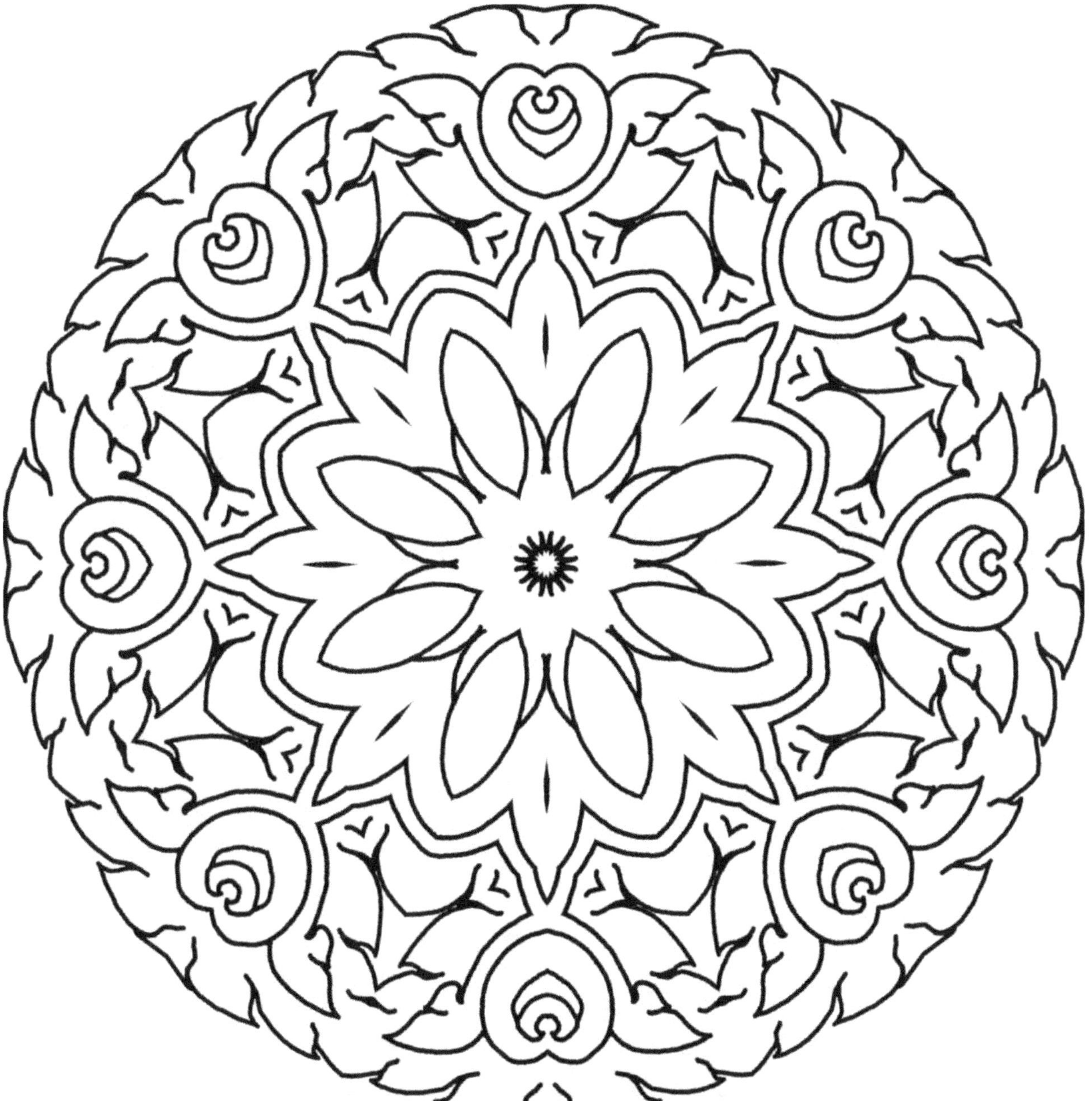

Thank you

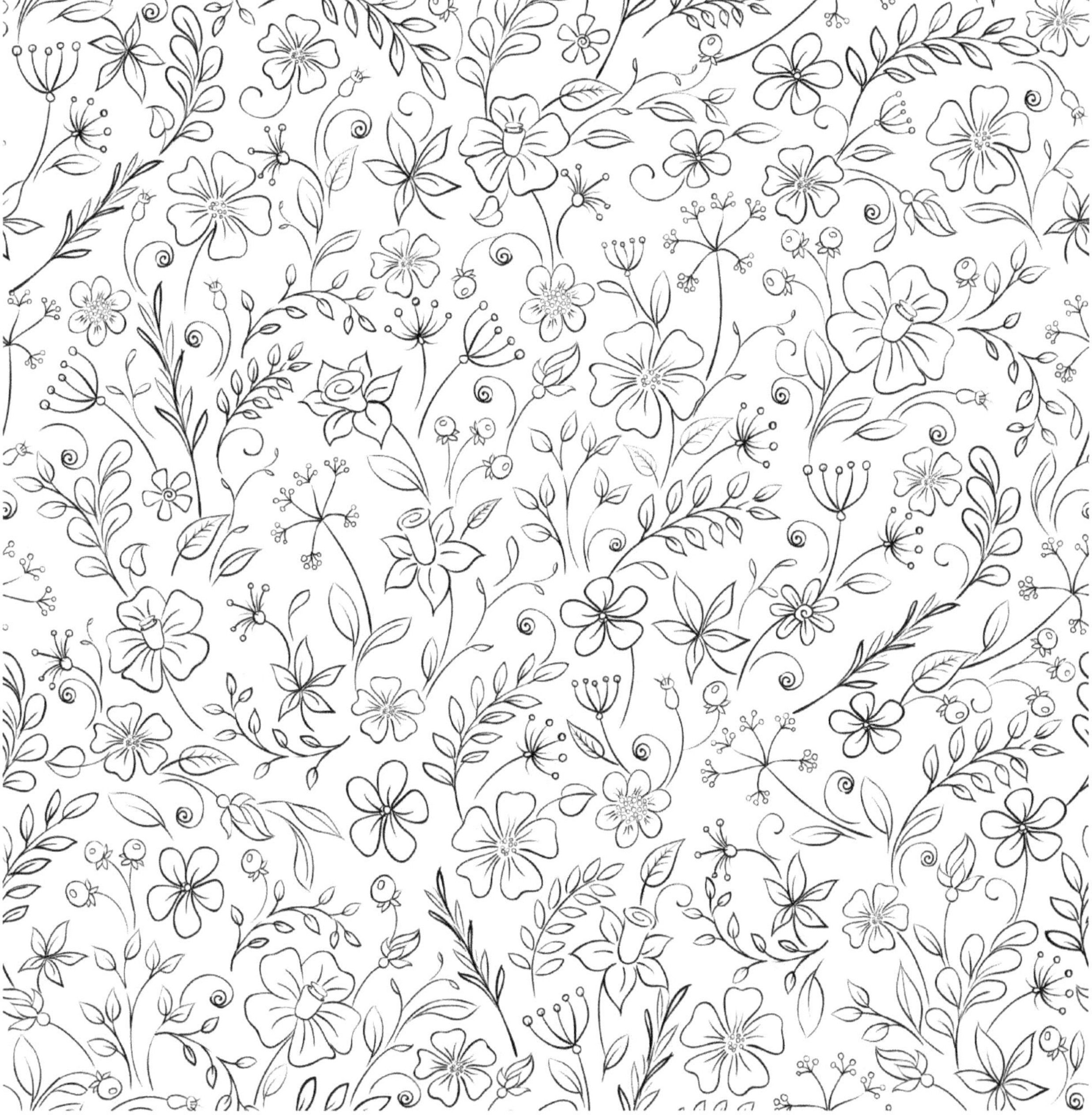

www.ingramcontent.com/pod-product-compliance
Lightning Source LLC
Chambersburg PA
CBHW081115180526
45170CB00008B/2848
9781542520225